Living in Real Time

COURTNEY ROBISON-DIXON

Living in
Real Time

COURTNEY ROBISON-DIXON

Photographs of the author on the front and back covers
were provided courtesy of Paula Blackwood.

ISBN: 978-1-953058-14-0

Printed in the United States of America

Book design by Scott Stortz

Published by:
Butler Books
(502) 897–9393
info@butlerbooks.com
www.butlerbooks.com

IN LOVING MEMORY OF

LESLEY & RHYAN
PRATHER

CARRIE & KACEY
McCAW

YOUR KIVA FAMILY LOVES & MISSES YOU.

To my four angels:

I love you. I miss you.

I live to not let your legacy die.

About Courtney

Courtney Robison-Dixon is a former Division I volleyball player at the University of Louisville who turned a passion for volleyball into a full-time career. Over the past ten years, Courtney has focused her athletic skills and energy on coaching and mentoring girls ages 10–18, as one of the directors of Kentucky Indiana Volleyball Academy (KIVA)—one of the most prominent and prestigious volleyball clubs in the country.

In 2016, Courtney was nominated by the American Volleyball Coaches Association for the "30 under 30 Award," solidifying her reputation as one of the most sought-after young coaches in the country. Her passion to inspire young women to excel as athletes, and to become confident women who value themselves and believe in their power to impact the world in a positive way, is the catalyst that brought this book to life.

Courtney lives in Southern Indiana with her husband Will. Her life reflects the same goals and mission statement she recommends to the young women she mentors: *Find your passion, make it your life's purpose, and live it in a positive and powerful way.*

Contents

Introduction

"I am convinced that life is 10% what happens to me and 90% how I react to it. And so it is with you. We are in charge of our attitudes."

—*Charles Swindoll*

Unfortunately, we live in a world that is governed by social media through false images of expectations of how we are "supposed" to live and what we are supposed to look like. The false realities that media today portrays are accompanied by a societal mindset and desire of instant gratification and convenience. Everybody wants their issues and problems solved instantly. They want their lives to be made as convenient as possible, where they put in little effort to complete daily tasks. Due to our evolving society, individuals get lost in their daily worlds of convenience and distractions. They have forgotten and lost sight of the beauty and true essence of life.

The purpose of this book is to help young women learn the dangers of the false reality society tries to portray. The goal of the information that lies ahead is for adolescents to learn to live in *real time*, not behind the stress and anxiety of a social media timeline.

This book will help show you that we are women of strength,

power, and beauty from the inside out. It is my hope that the pages that follow will help you realize you have dignity and worth.

This journey that you are on, called life, is 100% within your control, no matter how small or powerless you feel at this moment. I hope that as you dive deeper into this book, it reveals to you the strengths and talents that you have, and that you then use them as a platform to inspire others. You are in a period of your life that is so influential on the woman you will be down the road. This phase is extremely foundational in setting your morals and beliefs. It is in your adolescent years that you begin to make impactful decisions, establish a work ethic, learn time management, and understand teamwork, just to name a few things. The qualities and traits girls develop during their teenage years help mold them into the wives, mothers, and leaders in society they will become.

What you do now matters. The decisions you make now will impact your future. The people you choose to associate with, or not to associate with, will influence who you are. The habits you develop now will stick with you in your 20s, 30s, and so on. The romantic relationships you entertain now are helping you to become a better wife for your future husband.

It is my hope that this book will help you realize that money, fame, and Instagram likes do not provide true happiness. True happiness comes from the genuine relationships we have that make us whole. True happiness comes from the strength and confidence we gain from the accomplishments we achieve and the success we have. True happiness comes from the love we are shown by those closest to us in our lives. True happiness does *not* come from how many followers we have on Twitter, or from the number of Snapchat streaks we have, or from the number of likes on our last Insta post.

This book will help you find true happiness and understand how to be present in this beautiful world, in real time, in real life. It will help you separate yourself from the darkness, negativity, and anxiety of social acceptance via social media. Through these pages, it is my hope that you will be inspired to see what your true passion is, understand your purpose, and have the strength and courage to influence others in a powerful and positive way.

Part One

Your Relationships

CHAPTER ONE

Living in Real Time

>∽♡∽

"The hardest challenge is to be yourself in a world where everyone is trying to make you be somebody else."

—E. E. Cummings

"Should I post the picture at 3:00 pm, right when everyone gets out of school? Or do I wait until 9:00 pm? When will everyone be on their phones? I want to get the most likes possible on this picture!"

"Hey guys, come here. Let's do a boomerang for my story!"

"I hate her! She only posted that picture because she looks good and I look horrible."

"You know she is only posting that to make sure I know she's with him."

"Which filter makes me look skinny and tan?"

"I've only gotten 100 likes on this pic. Should I delete it?"

These are all comments we have said and heard our peers say. Whether we want to admit it or not, we live in a world and society driven by social media. 95% of US teens have access to a smartphone, and all of these teens report they use social media.

Teenage girls live in a world where social acceptance is driven by a *timeline*. You wake up before school and immediately check Instagram to see if the queen bee of your school has posted a picture of herself and her boyfriend. Or you tap on every story to see if any of the popular girls posted an OOTD (outfit of the day), hoping you can come up with something similar, only to be left disheartened because you can't afford the expensive clothes they wear and the bags they carry.

You get out of school, and what do you do? Go right to Snapchat, only to be disappointed he didn't snap you back. Before you go to bed, you are back to scrolling aimlessly through the timelines, telling yourself you are not pretty enough, skinny enough, wealthy enough, or athletic enough in comparison to all the girls on your feed.

You spend your entire day in a virtual world where everyone seems perfect and so far from what you could ever be. You compare yourself daily, over and over, resulting in feelings of loneliness, inadequacy, and even depression.

If I could only get to 1,000 followers, I would finally be happy.

If I can get this picture to 500 likes, maybe he will finally notice me and ask me to the dance.

Keep in mind 90% of your followers are fake friends with whom you have had fewer than five face-to-face conversations. Even worse, some of those followers you have *never* spoken to in real life.

Young women believe a new follower notification, or their picture having more likes than someone else's, or a Snapchat streak with that hot guy, is what drives their inner happiness. However, is our social media identity really what creates happiness?

I am going to challenge you to do something. Think back to two scenarios I know we have all experienced at one point as a teenage girl.

Scenario One

You were on a beach trip with your best friend for spring break, and the two of you took at least 50 photos in the same bathing suits and with the same background, just switching up poses to find the perfect one. Then you sorted through all those images for hours, deleting the bad ones and saving the ones you thought were Instagram-worthy.

Finally, on a Tuesday night at 9:30, the timing is right. Everyone is on their phones, and you are sure to get *so many* likes on this picture. You upload the perfect one, do some editing to make sure your legs look a little thinner and your hips a little more narrow, find the perfect filter to make you look like a bronze goddess, insert that clever caption of "Sexy and slaying in the sand," and finally hit "post."

For a second, your stomach plummets as you worry: Will the popular girls think your caption is lame? Will all the guys at school think you're way too fat to post a bikini pic? You sit alone in your dark bedroom, the only light coming from the screen of your phone. At that very second, as you wait for the social acceptance or ridicule to begin, you've never felt so vulnerable, weak, or alone.

Then, seconds later, notifications of likes and comments begin to flood your screen. People are posting comments with emoji flames below your image. Finally, you are able to take a breath. At 11:00 pm, you're still alone in your bedroom, but at that moment you feel a sense of happiness, love, and social acceptance showered over you by your social media friends in cyberspace.

Scenario Two

It's a Friday night in the fall, after a home football game. You and your girlfriends are sitting on the floor in your bedroom. It's one o'clock in the morning. All of you are wearing sweatpants and T-shirts, with no makeup on. Pizza boxes are spread out in front of you, and your mom made homemade brownies that you can't get enough of.

You're going around telling stories about what happened at the game, talking about which couple was holding hands or which girls were wearing sweatshirts with the names of their football player boyfriends on the back.

Then, all of a sudden, one of you farts in the middle of a story. In a split second, all of you completely forget about what anyone thinks of you. You are literally crying because you are laughing so hard.

Be honest with yourself and tell me: On which night in your bedroom did you have more fun? On which night did you feel more love, happiness, and acceptance? I'm going out on a limb and saying every one of you enjoyed the carefree Friday night— the night you were able to be your complete self—over the Tuesday evening you spent alone and anxious as to whether your Instagram post would be accepted by your peers.

You chose the Friday night because in that moment you were experiencing genuine face-to-face communication, connection, and acceptance. Unfortunately, I promise you that no matter how many followers you have or how many likes you receive, a screen will never be able to give you the happiness and satisfaction that the present time can provide.

Do not let social media create your identity. The images you see and the profiles you view online, from celebrities to the girl next door, have all been edited, altered, and manipulated to portray a perfect life, body, boyfriend, and so on. Not a single thing you see online is an authentic reality of someone's true self. The images are created, edited, and branded to market a false but perfect version of that person for the cyber world.

So stop comparing your body, clothes, and travel experiences to those of the celebrities and peers on your timeline. Put an end to your identity being based on what people view on a screen. Make the choice now to stop living your life on a social media *timeline* and to start living in *real time*.

Go to the mall with your friends without making videos for your stories the entire time you are there. Go to dinner with your family without making a boomerang of your food to post. Go on a date and leave your phone in the car. Actually enjoy the experience in real time, with face-to-face conversation, instead of worrying about the best spot for taking a picture you can post to social media later that night. Be where your feet are. Enjoy the present: it's called the present because it is a gift.

I will never forget my very first date with my now-husband, Will. I was 24. It was a triple date with our sisters and their husbands, who had all been friends for years. This was the first time I'd ever formally met Will. As we drove to the restaurant for dinner, we made small talk. You know the kind of starter conversation where you are awkwardly trying to get to know someone? Yeah, that. Awkward, but fun. Things were going well. I was enjoying his company and was excited to see where the rest of the date took us.

When we arrived at the restaurant, Will parked the car. What happened next is a moment I will never forget. He lifted the center console of his truck and placed his phone inside. He then exited the truck. I was in shock as I tried to collect myself. I hustled out of the truck quickly as well and asked him, "Do you not need to take your phone with you?"

Seeming confused by my question, Will responded genuinely, "I'm with you tonight. Why would I need my phone?"

This moment on our first date was life-changing for me, and not only because it was the first night I met my now-husband. It was a reality check for me in regard to what matters most in life: Being present. Enjoying the moment. Living life in real time and not on a social media timeline.

Take this advice from a girl who spent hours scrolling and comparing herself to others. Take it from a girl who debated for hours whether a given picture and caption were worth posting. Take it from a girl who thought happiness and success in high school and even college was gauged by the number of likes. Trust me when I tell you that true happiness and identity are not found on a timeline. The uniqueness of you is created in real time, through true-life experiences, interacting face to face with people of all races, religions, and moral values. True happiness comes from solving real-life problems and overcoming obstacles so that you can achieve genuine accomplishments and success.

Each of you has beauty, strength, power, and confidence, even if you can't see it right now. My hope for you is that by the end of this book, you can identify yourself as a beautiful and strong woman through life experiences and personal relationships that are all guided by your morals and values. I challenge you to look at your beauty from the inside out. See the light that shines from deep within your soul and heart, not from what is seen through a screen.

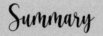
Summary

- Every picture you see on social media is carefully edited to create a "picture-perfect" image for the cyber world.
- True happiness comes in the present time, with real-life people, developing true relationships, not from social media likes.
- Live in real time, not on a timeline.

friendships

~♡~

"As you grow older, you realize it becomes less important to have more friends and more important to have real ones."

—Ziad K. Abdelnour

"Some friends are like pennies: two-faced and worthless."

—Author unknown

As one transitions from elementary to middle school, from middle to high school, and from high school to college, one scary constant remains: the fear of trying to make new friends. We have all experienced this fear at some point in our lives.

As you make a transition to a new school, you think about what to wear on the first day to get the popular girls to think you are cool. Thoughts of how to look cute enough to catch the eyes of the hot guys flood your brain. You have already done the research to see who is in your classes, who is dating whom, and which outfits and purses are socially acceptable. You have spent hours on social media, hoping to become friends with *that group of girls* or get in with *that clique*.

But I am about to break some truth to you. It can't be found in a school textbook, and your teachers will probably never lecture on it. However, as Muhammad Ali once said, "Friendship is the hardest thing in the world to explain. It's not something you learn in school. But if you haven't learned the meaning of friendship, you really haven't learned anything."

True friends are the ones you can call at any time of day, the ones you spend hours sitting and talking with, the ones you can see in person without worrying about putting concealer on that pimple to hide it. These are the people who will love and support you no matter how many social media followers or likes you have.

You will spend your adolescent years trying to navigate who your real friends are. You will sort through fake friends who just want to be friends with you for various reasons, such as your parents having a lot of money, or your house having a pool, or you owning cute clothes that the fake friends want to borrow. You will spend your teenage years thinking, *Wow, this girl could be my lifelong best friend*, only to find out a week later that she started a rumor about you.

Here's the good news, though: All of the drama, humiliation, and fake friendships you go through in these years are not a bad thing, if looked at and handled from the right perspective. Every friendship you have in your adolescent years not only helps you to identify the personality traits and qualities you want and expect from a friend, but it helps you determine the characteristics you want to exhibit toward your own friends.

Do not look at fake or failed friendships as wasted time in your life. Each of these interactions is monumental in creating what I like to call your *friendship bank*.

Try to imagine your friendships as debits and credits from your banking account. When fake friends betray or abandon you, they take your trust, companionship, and love. In doing this, they take a withdrawal from your friendship bank. However, while they punch out a debit, you actually gain a credit. Picture this: When you purchase a dress, you have to withdraw money from your account, but you gain the result of now owning that dress. When your former friend withdraws from your friendship bank, you gain the credit of knowledge and understanding of the qualities and characteristics you do *not* want in your future friends.

When we are lucky enough to be blessed with those few friends who are 100% loyal to us, they will love us when we are at our highest in life and when we are broken into a thousand pieces. They will always be there, no matter what. These friends are like deposits or investments. They are constantly adding value to our friendship banks and our lives as a whole.

It is important to understand that not every person you hang out with will be a true best friend. That's okay. There are two types of friends we have in our lives: *surface friends* and *deep friends*.

Surface friends are friends who share similar hobbies with you, or maybe you live on the same street. You occasionally interact based on that proximity. These friends are very nice and fun to hang out with, but you would never tell them your deepest fears or secrets.

Deep friends are those few close friends who know everything about you. They know the good, the bad, and the ugly, and they still love you. These are the friends you can have profound conversations with. You can go to them when your heart is broken over some guy who didn't deserve you in the first place. You can go to them when your parents are fighting so much that you don't even want to live in your own home. You can go to them when you feel you do not fit in anywhere.

These are your girls. These are your ride-or-dies. Trust me, when you find them, you know it, and you do not want to let them go. Love those girls unconditionally. Be the friend to them that you would want. Be loyal to them. When people talk bad about them, stick up for them, even though facing conflict head-on is one of the hardest things to do in life.

It is so easy to sit back and remain silent when people talk bad about others. You will face this often in your adolescent years. On the inside, you will rage with anger, because the things being said are not true. However, fear of being ridiculed will tell you to just keep your mouth shut and try to be invisible.

This situation is very difficult; there are adults who still struggle with it. However, my challenge to you is to dig deep into your soul and have the strength to speak up for your friends. Defend them. I promise, once you get those first words out, it will get easier from there. Once you have said your piece, you are going to feel so proud of yourself for not only facing conflict head-on but for being loyal to your friends.

When I was a senior in high school, my best friend Katie—who is still my best friend to this day—was a junior. Katie was beautiful, smart, athletic, and successful. Every guy in town wanted to date her. Naturally, due to Katie's beauty and success, many girls in my class did not like her.

At a party one weekend, several classmates I had thought of as friends were talking bad about Katie. Internally I was furious, but I was so scared to say anything. A million thoughts were going through my head:

Go ahead and speak. You have to stick up for her.

Don't do it. Everyone will laugh at you.

Just walk away and act like you didn't hear them.

As my armpits and palms began to sweat, I finally cleared my throat and said, "Hey, all of those things you guys are saying about Katie aren't true. You don't even know her."

It felt like five minutes passed in dead silence as I sat there waiting for their response. Again, thoughts flooded my head:

Are they going to laugh at me?

Are they going to stand up and punch me in the face?

Maybe they didn't hear me, and this is my chance to run away.

Then, all of a sudden, the queen bee of the group stood up and said, "Let's go, ladies. No reason to hang out with her."

And they all walked away.

As I gathered a breath of relief, my initial thought was, *Thank God they didn't beat me up.* But then I realized that while standing there all alone in the middle of that party, I had never felt so strong, powerful, and proud as I did in that moment.

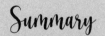
Summary

- Every friendship adds to your friendship bank.
- Every backstabbing friend, lost friendship, and betrayal shapes the expectations you have for your friends and how you treat others.
- Surface friends are your everyday acquaintances.
- Deep friends are your ride-or-dies.

CHAPTER THREE

Bullying

~♡~

*"Cyberbullying **is** bullying. Hiding behind a pretty screen doesn't make it less hateful. Written words have power."*

—Author unknown

"Not all forms of abuse leave bruises."

—Danielle Steel

Unfortunately, ladies, we all know it: Girls can be cruel. You will experience and see more vicious behavior and bullying in your adolescent years than during any other period in your life. Each of you at some point will probably be a victim of bullying, and you may be tempted to be a perpetrator too. My hope is that you will be strong in your morals and not take part in the malicious world of bullying.

Through my years of coaching youth athletes, I have witnessed at first hand face-to-face bullying and cyberbullying. Below are just a few of the situations I have encountered:

- Making a list of girls on a team and rating them from "prettiest" to "ugliest"

- Telling one girl she can't come to the party because none of the boys in class think she is pretty
- Countless texts and social media posts ridiculing one individual
- Creating group chats and purposely excluding one person
- Telling one girl that the party is at a particular location when really it is elsewhere. That girl shows up at the fake location and no one is there. The other girls then send her a text saying "LOL, guess no one wanted to hang out with you . . . they moved the party somewhere else!"
- Telling someone the party was canceled when it wasn't and then taking social media pictures/videos and posting them for the girl who was excluded to see

I have sat in my office for hours upon hours as beautiful young women share such stories with me. Tears fill their eyes and their voices shake as they try to speak in between the sniffles and gasps for breath. I look at these young women, so beautiful inside and out. They are intelligent and athletic and have so much life ahead of them. Yet they feel broken. Many feel, at that moment, that the world would be a better place without them. Some of them have even told me that if they were not on this Earth, they would no longer be in pain. Let me hit you with a real hard truth, ladies: 6,800 American teenagers committed suicide in 2018.

One of the leading drivers for suicide is bullying that leads to depression. It is easy to make fun of someone, especially when others are doing it too. It is even easier to type a mean or threatening text or post when you are protected by a screen. However, before you say that hurtful comment to someone or before you make that mean post about someone, think back to the 6,800 teens who committed suicide in 2018.

I know what you are thinking right now: *Yeah, I've heard of kids committing suicide because they were bullied, but that wouldn't happen to anyone I know. I'd never make fun of someone that much anyway.* But what you say to or about someone, even if it seems like a small thing, could be the final straw that breaks him or her. You never know where someone is, mentally and emotionally, at any moment in time. The saying "sticks and stones will break my bones, but words will never hurt me" isn't true. Words are weapons that chip away at someone's self-esteem. Your words may be the last chip.

Bullying, including cyberbullying, is very real. I can promise you, it is taking place in your hometown, in your school, on your teams, and in your social groups. You may not see it right now, but it is there, and it is serious.

When bullying does happen, you have two choices:

Stand By

or

Stand Up

Stand by and do nothing, and you are a bully yourself. This includes reading bullying social media posts and not doing anything about them. Do not stand by and allow someone to be hurt, possibly even to become the next suicide statistic.

Instead, stand up for those who are being bullied. Be the bigger person and make the harder choice for those who are being ridiculed. Defend them and put the bully in his or her place. Then tell a trusted adult, such as a parent, teacher, counselor, or coach, who can take action to prevent future bullying.

Sometimes, the bullies may turn their sights on you. Most people are bullied at some time in their lives. If so, *you are not alone*. Do not be afraid or embarrassed; millions of people suffer from bullying every day! And do not try to fight this horrible cycle on your own. Tell a trusted adult what you are facing. I promise they can help and protect you. They can give you the love you have been longing for.

Realize you are more beautiful even than what you see in the mirror. You are smarter than you give yourself credit for. You are braver than you believe, and you are stronger than you think. You are a woman of power. Use it. Make the decision to get your happy life back under your control.

The reality is that people only put others down because of their own insecurities. Bullies are not happy with their own lives, so to make themselves feel better, they put others down who they feel *are* happy. Bullies target people they are envious of. Whether they are jealous of a person's appearance, athleticism, social status, or wealth, a bully will always try to tear them down.

It is important to remember this, because you will face it throughout your life. In your 20s, people are envious of what college you got into, or what job you got, or whom you are marrying. Bullies will envy these accomplishments of yours and try to belittle you. In your 30s and 40s, people will be spiteful about the achievements of you, your spouse, or your children, and they will ridicule you and your family.

Jealousy is a vicious disease many people suffer with all their lives. Let people's jealousy of you allow you to thrive. Let it be fuel to your fire, and allow it to make you successful. Take every knock as a compliment to the bully's belief that you are a complete *badass*. Remember, they are only knocking you down because you are already higher up than they are. They wish they were you: smart, beautiful, and successful. Let their envy drive you to continue to achieve great things!

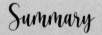

- Bullying can be found in many forms: mental, emotional, physical, and sexual abuse.
- Bullying can cause dramatic consequences. Remember, 6,800 American teenagers committed suicide due to bullying in just one year.
- Stand up for those being bullied. If you stand by and remain silent, you are just as guilty as the individual who is bullying.
- If you're being bullied, don't be afraid to ask for help.
- Remember: you are not alone.

CHAPTER FOUR

Confidence

∿♡∿

"The most beautiful thing you can wear is confidence."
—Blake Lively

I have a very good friend whom I would consider a deep friend. Ours is one of those friendships where we can discuss family, religion, and politics, and even when we agree to disagree on some things, we still love each other. Married for 17 years and a business owner for 19 years, Jim is an individual I have looked up to as a mentor in life and in business. He has shared with me great wisdom on how to love and lead others.

One evening, in a deep conversation about life and business, he said to me, "Courtney, the most beautiful trait a woman has is her confidence."

I remember going home that night and pondering the comment. At first, it didn't make sense to me. Normally, we think of the most attractive parts of a female as her beautiful sun-kissed skin, or maybe her long blonde hair or her sparkling green eyes. I thought to myself, *How in the world is confidence seen as visually beautiful?* I was intrigued and needed further explanation, so I asked Jim to

25

meet me for lunch.

As we sat there, I told him his comment had been on my mind for a while now and I needed him to explain it in more depth. I expressed that I didn't understand how a woman's confidence could be beautiful. Jim just laughed. He took a drink of his water, set down his glass, and took a deep breath. Then he leaned forward and began to speak.

He explained that a woman who is firm in her foundation, has strong morals, and lives her life by a set of values is proud of the person she is. A woman who is true to who she is can face obstacles and overcome them without letting fear or anxiety get in the way. When a girl walks into the room with her shoulders back, head held high, and a big smile on her face, she immediately demands attention and respect from everyone in the room. She doesn't have to say a word; her body language speaks for itself. The way she carries herself in confidence radiates beauty to all around her.

As I sat there and listened to him speak, it was as if he were giving me the winning numbers to a lottery ticket. It all made sense, and I realized he couldn't have been more right. All I wanted to do was run back to all my athletes and yell, "Girls, just be confident and you will be beautiful!"

However, as I drove back to work from lunch that day, I knew it was not that simple.

Confidence is something every teenage girl struggles with every day. In fact, confidence is something every human being battles, no matter what age, gender, or ethnicity. The famous actresses, athletes, and authors you and I both idolize encounter confidence issues daily as well. It is human nature. We all struggle with it.

Take myself, for example. I struggled with the confidence to write and publish this book. I've always thought of myself as a confident woman, but the thought of putting my thoughts and beliefs into words for people to read was terrifying. I second-guessed myself for a long time before I finally got the courage to begin writing, and I had moments of doubt throughout the writing, editing, and publishing process. I feared no publisher would take this on, or that no one would read it, or even that people would laugh at me. I feared that I would fail.

However, I relied on my self-confidence deep within to continue to encourage me to write. I knew that if I could get this book published, it would end up in the hands of at least one young girl like yourself, and that was all that mattered.

Having confidence when you're a teenager is especially tough. So many things in a teenage girl's world are changing: new schools, new friends, new boyfriends, a period. (Seriously, periods are gross. Why do we have to have them?) Heck, we even have new pimples every day! I mean, how is a girl supposed to be confident when there's a mountain on her face the size of Mount Everest and blood pouring from her like Niagara Falls? All you want to do is crawl into a cave and never come out!

Tell me you haven't felt like this before. I know you've been there; we all have. That's what you have to remember: we have *all* been there!

You are not battling alone this crazy thing we call life. Everything you are experiencing and feel embarrassed about, your best friend has felt at some point. That queen bee of your school has gone through it too, and yes, so have all the famous Instagram models. They might not post about it, but they were teenage girls once too. You may think they look confident, but usually they're faking it. They know the confidence struggle. They have lived it. Many of them still suffer with confidence issues today.

Confidence is built from the inside out. However, sometimes it is easier to be reminded of our confidence from the outside in.

Let me explain this concept. An individual's confidence is built on his or her foundation. This foundation is created through one's values, beliefs, and morals. Together, these qualities govern every decision and action. The results of these actions generate successes or failures. Positive results typically reinforce confidence, while failures decrease it.

Ultimately, when we live our lives through strong ethics, that leads us to have great friends, achievements, and happiness. However, sometimes it is difficult to just think about ourselves as confident individuals who have achieved great things. Every single one of us could make a list of 20 things right now that are "wrong with us" or that we can't do. We might wish we looked like this or wish we had that. We could come up with an endless list of all the negative things associated with who we are. However, I guarantee we would all struggle to list five positive qualities or achievements we have. Why is this? As humans, and especially as females, we are quick to judge ourselves in a negative light. We never give ourselves credit where credit is due.

A trick that I want to teach you is to look at yourself from the outside in. In other words, look at your achievements: the A you got on the last test, the role in the spring play, the team you finally made, the song you can finally play on the guitar after working so hard to learn it, the awards you have achieved. When you feel as if you have lost all confidence—or when you feel as if you never had any to begin with—I challenge you to write these achievements down on a piece of paper. Tape them to your bathroom mirror or inside your planner, somewhere you will see them every day. These are the black and white facts proving you are smart, talented, and successful. These are the truths of your life. They will remind you of all the reasons why you *should* be confident in the young woman you are!

Confidence is beautiful, and it is very much noticeable. Think about it. We have all watched a beautiful girl walk past us in the mall with her head held high, huge smile on her face, hips going side to side with every step as her long, gorgeous brown hair sways in unison with them. We look at her and think, *Dang, she is so beautiful and looks so confident in who she is.* We immediately envy her.

Confidence is the most valuable and beautiful trait you hold as a woman. Ladies, the sooner you realize this and embrace it, the sooner you will experience power over your life and find ultimate happiness and success.

Confidence is a key pillar in creating the strongest version of you. You must learn to love yourself before you can have any true friendships or romantic relationships. Your ability to love yourself and be confident in who you are builds the expectations you set for how your future friends and romantic partners will treat you.

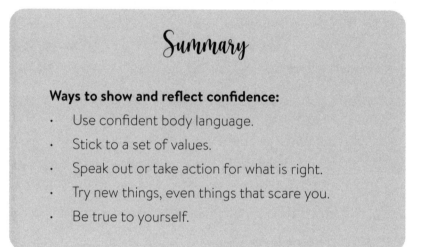

Summary

Ways to show and reflect confidence:
- Use confident body language.
- Stick to a set of values.
- Speak out or take action for what is right.
- Try new things, even things that scare you.
- Be true to yourself.

CHAPTER FIVE

Love

"First love is only a little foolishness and a lot of curiosity."
—*George Bernard Shaw*

"Young love is a flame; very pretty, often very hot and fierce, but still only light and flickering. The love of the older and disciplined heart is as coals, deep-burning, unquenchable."
—*Henry Ward Beecher*

"All my friends have boyfriends except me. I'm literally the third wheel everywhere I go."
—*Katelyn, age 15*

"OMG . . . we have snapped 100 days straight, he for sure loves me."
—*Blakynn, age 14*

"We have dated for two years. I know we will stay together even though we are going to different colleges. We have even talked about getting married after college."

—*Brooke, age 18*

The stories above have been told to me during my years of working with adolescents. If I'm being honest with you, I myself even thought or said those same things when I was a teenager. By looking back on my own adolescent years, speaking with teenagers today, and picking the brains of women in their 20s, 30s, 40s, and beyond, I hope I can provide you some insight and hope on the issue of love during your teenage years. Unfortunately, no textbook or class lecture will share with you the knowledge and wisdom you need to navigate love as a teenager. However, I truly believe the information that lies ahead will help direct you through the process with strength, courage, and confidence.

In this chapter we will discuss the following points in regard to teenage romantic relationships:

- Love yourself before you let a guy love you.
- Do not change for a guy.
- Demand respect.
- Don't ditch your friends.
- Heartbreak equals strength.

Love yourself before you let a guy love you

Before any romantic relationship can take place, you must know who you are, be confident in who you are, and love the woman you are. Each of us grows mentally, physically, emotionally, and spiritually throughout our lives. However, one thing must always remain as we are growing: We must love and be happy with the woman we are.

One of the biggest mistakes you can make as a teenager is to be in a state of low self-esteem and seek love, happiness, and confidence through a romantic relationship. Of course, you want any person you are dating to make you laugh and feel happy and to give you compliments. However, you must be happy with yourself first. You want the romantic relationship to add to your jar of happiness—not to be the first pour.

Teenage girls who are battling with self-esteem issues are very sensitive and vulnerable. Vulnerability leads to poor decision-making. Oftentimes, teenage girls who seek to fill a self-confidence void through the avenue of a romantic relationship are pressured into unwanted sexual activity.

Before you make the mistake of using a romantic relationship as a way to gain love, happiness, and confidence, think again. Remember who you are. Remember the morals and values you have based your life on up to this point. Whether you believe it or not, I am here to tell you that you are a beautiful, strong, intelligent, successful young woman. You are a young woman of dignity and worth. You *do not* have to give a guy anything you do

33

not want to just to try to achieve happiness and acceptance. If a boy truly cares for you and loves you for who you are, he will never ask you to do something you are uncomfortable doing. If he does, he is not the right guy for you. Move on until you find someone who respects you for who you are and what you stand for.

Do not change for a guy

Many teenage girls find the first weeks of a romantic relationship super exciting and fun. The flirty text messages, Friday night football games together, and late-night phone calls keep you living on a romantic high. Unfortunately, the "honeymoon" phase will soon wear off, and so often, guys will then start trying to control their girlfriends.

> "He won't let me go to the movies with you guys because he is out of town this weekend. He doesn't want me there without him."
> —Sasha, age 16

> "He told me I should run more because it would make my thighs less thick."
> —Kendall, age 19

> "He said I need to wear more V-neck shirts so he can see my boobs better."
> —Skylar, age 15

Unfortunately, I have heard countless stories like these. I remember them from my own teenage years, I've had my teenage athletes share them with me, and I've heard them from mothers of adolescents all over the country.

This is from the women who have gone before you, who have lived the very difficult teenage life you are in right now: *Be strong in your morals.* Be confident in who you are. Do *not* change for a guy. Do not let anyone tell you that you are not pretty enough, skinny enough, or smart enough. Realize that the behavior you accept from a guy when you are an adolescent builds the foundation of what you will look for and accept in future relationships. Think about it. Do you want your future husband to tell you that you are inadequate? To try to change the way you look or dress?

Do yourself and your future children a favor: Do not allow a man to change you or control you. Wait for the guy who appreciates you for the person you are, the guy who doesn't want to change a thing about you or what you look like. Trust me, beautiful: You are perfect just the way you are.

Demand respect

The concepts of chivalry and of being a Southern gentleman seem to be dying off with each generation, but they are not yet extinct. In fact, as teenage girls, you have the most power of any women right now to bring these charming concepts of manhood back to life! The adolescent years are some of the most fun and memorable years in regard to beliefs and behaviors of love. Do you want that fairytale love story where Prince Charming sweeps you off your feet and then you ride away together and live happily ever after? Well, ladies, make it happen twenty-first–century style. The power is in your hands to bring out that Prince Charming in today's teenage boys.

How do you do it, you ask? Demand respect. Demand that your boyfriends treat you like the princess you are. Let me give you some examples:

- Make him ask you to be his girlfriend in a face-to-face conversation, not through a phone call, text, snapchat, or DM.
- Make him open the car door for you. You will only have to ask him in a flirty, cute way once, and I guarantee he will do it from then on out.
- Tell him sometimes that you love when he tells you you're beautiful or gorgeous, not just hot.

Do not mistake these for signs of a woman being submissive to a man. These are all just simple, traditional gestures of respect in a relationship. Always remember, in any relationship, you are an equal to the man. You should never feel belittled, weaker, or less than he in any way. With that being said, always remember you should show him respect, just as you expect it from him.

As you begin your dating life, you may have several boyfriends before you find your forever soulmate. As you experience each of these relationships, always have respect for yourself by staying true to your morals. However, also demand respect from your partner. Remember that you are an independent woman and you can care for yourself with or without a man. As you journey through your adolescent years and into your 20s, it is imperative that you remember never to put yourself into a situation where you are forced to be dependent on a man mentally, emotionally, or financially. Always be able to support yourself. Build mental and emotional strength through your values and confidence. Get your education and a career that can financially provide for you.

Then, years down the road, when you find your soulmate and look him in the eyes while you say "I do," he will be so proud to know his wife is a strong and independent woman who will teach their future children how to follow in her footsteps.

Don't ditch your friends

Either you've done it or one of your friends has done it to you: a girl gets a boyfriend and goes MIA for months, never comes to girls' nights anymore, doesn't text her friends back because she is always on the phone with her boyfriend. Don't make this mistake. Trust me, I get it: When you get a boyfriend, you are head over heels, butterflies in your stomach, daydreaming over him all the time. Yes, it is exciting. However, do not let it consume you.

It is important, as you enter this new phase of dating, to have balance. Balance your time, efforts, and energy. Just because you have a boyfriend now doesn't mean you can forget about your faith, school, family, job (if you have one), sports, theatre, clubs, and so on. Life is all about balance, regardless of how old you are.

However, your adolescent years are your first true test of time management and balance, especially when it comes to dating.

As you are falling head over heels for your new boo, try to remember who has been there for you long before this guy: your family and friends. It is okay to be excited about your new relationship, and it is okay to spend time with this person. However, you need to make time to spend with your family and friends as well, because nine times out of ten, this is not going to be the guy you marry. Chances are, in a year you won't even talk to him. I know it is hard to believe that right now, but the statistics speak for themselves: only 2% of high school relationships result in marriage.

So don't turn your back and ditch the people who will actually be there on your wedding day, when you finally do marry Prince Charming.

Heartbreak equals strength

According to researchers at the Institute for Family Studies, only 25% of women state that they married their first love. That means the other 75% of women experienced a breakup, usually during their adolescent and early adult years. The reality of teenage romantic relationships is that the majority of them end in one or both parties being heartbroken. If you have not experienced your first heartbreak, consider yourself lucky. But there's probably one in your future, and hopefully this book will help you be mentally prepared for when it does occur.

For you ladies who have had your heart ripped out of your chest and sat on the couch for two days in your pajamas eating from a gallon tub of chocolate chip cookie dough ice cream while watching "The Notebook" as tears rolled down your face, I wish I could come wrap my arms around you and embrace you right now. There is no pain like heartbreak, especially your first one.

When you experience a heartbreak, you truly feel as if your world has come crashing down on top of you. You feel there is no way your life will go on. You tell yourself, *We had all the same friends; I'll never be able to show my face again!* You thought you two were going to get married; now you tell yourself, *I will never have a husband. I'll never get over him.*

These are all things girls have thought or said at some point during a catastrophic heartbreak. In that moment of pain, you do not think you will ever experience companionship, love, or happiness again. I've been there, girl. I had nine boyfriends before marrying my Prince Charming, and five of those nine relationships happened during my teenage years. Sometimes I was the one left crying on the couch. Sometimes I broke things off because I realized the boy did not have the qualities and traits I expected in a romantic partner.

With age and wisdom, I have learned that each of those relationships was monumental in shaping who I am as a wife today. None of those relationships do I regret or look at as wasted time. From each of those relationships I gained knowledge, experience, and understanding of what kind of man I wanted to marry and what characteristics I wanted to have as a wife one day. Most importantly, each one of those "failed" relationships led me one step closer to the arms of my loving husband.

Do not worry, girls! Your time will come. However, as with achieving anything great, you have to put in the dirty work first. You have to date all the wrong ones to realize which one is Mr. Right. You have to be treated like crap to see how incredibly "the one" really treats you. You have to have your heart shattered to realize what true love is when it finds you.

Wait for the man who, when you wake up in the morning in sweatpants and a T-shirt, hair on top of your head, wearing no makeup, smiles and says, "Good morning, beautiful. I love you." That's your Prince Charming, ladies. That's my husband, and I thank God every day that the others didn't work, because they led me to Will.

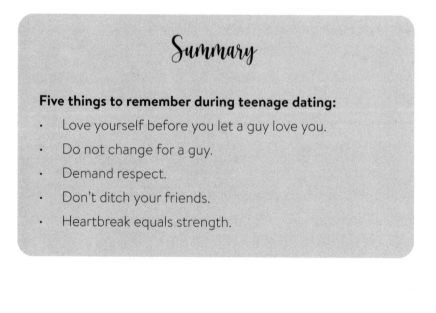

Summary

Five things to remember during teenage dating:
- Love yourself before you let a guy love you.
- Do not change for a guy.
- Demand respect.
- Don't ditch your friends.
- Heartbreak equals strength.

CHAPTER SIX

Sex

> "Does sex education encourage sex? Many parents are afraid that talking about sex with their teenagers will be taken as permission for the teen to have sex. Nothing could be further from the truth. If anything, the more children learn about sexuality from talking with their parents and teachers and reading accurate books, the less they feel compelled to find out for themselves."
>
> —Benjamin Spock

Sex is one of those topics that everyone thinks about, teenagers and adults. Yet it's that awkward elephant in the room, where no one discusses it.

As teenage girls, your hormones are all over the place. Your curiosity is through the roof. Peers who are all feeling the same way surround you. Even worse, your cell phones and Netflix pop up constant images that remind you of the sex-driven society we live in. With all these contributing factors, it is no surprise that so many teenagers want to experiment with sex. However, think of sex as a science experiment. You would never mix two chemicals together if you knew they would catch fire, explode, or cause damage to yourself or others in the lab, would you? No. The act of sex is no different during the teenage years.

You are at a point in your life where you walk the fine line of wanting to be an adult while in reality you're still a kid. You can't support yourself financially. You still need Mom and Dad to provide a roof over your head, food on the table, and clothes on your back. However, as a teenager you have your own morals and values, and you make a lot of your own choices. The independence and free will you are developing drives your feelings of believing you are an adult, making you believe you are ready to make adult decisions. But with adult decisions come adult consequences.

After interviewing many women of all ages, I've put together this list of a few points we wish we'd known regarding teenage sex.

- More than sex
- Emotional power of sex
- Make your husband proud
- Everlasting consequences

More than sex

Many females have the instinct to please, serve, and nurture others. It is natural. It is the motherly instinct that lies within us; we all have that in common. In many ways, this instinct helps make us wonderful individuals. It drives our compassion for others and helps us to care for and help those around us. It helps create the love we show to so many individuals in our lives. It will allow you to show compassion, love, and service to others throughout your life.

Unfortunately, there is a downfall to this natural instinct of wanting to please others. In our teenage years, we often think the only way we can give love and pleasure to a guy is through sex. We get caught up in wanting to make our partner happy, and we believe giving our body is the ultimate way for him to reach true happiness with us. However, take it from the many women who have gone before you, some who have made the mistake of giving themselves at a young age and some who have fought the temptation: you can give him more than sex.

Many of you may be asking yourselves right now, *How could I give him more than sex? That is all he wants.* Maybe it is, maybe it isn't. You would be surprised by the number of teenage guys who are just as nervous about the act as you are.

Instead of basing the relationship solely on sexual intercourse, learn to give someone more than your body. Learn to make him happy through your words, your acts of service toward him, the time you spend with him. By learning to show love in different ways at a young age, you are going to make your future relationships much more successful. Take it from many women who are now wives: your man wants to feel love in more ways than just what happens in the bedroom.

A lot of men desire the positive encouragement of a woman. They like hearing words of praise. So start with that. Start by constantly reminding your partner how handsome he is. Or how well he played in the football game last night. Or how proud you are of him for getting the lead role in the show. From there, learn how to bring your partner happiness through acts of kindness toward him. For example, make him dinner. Wash his car, if he has one. Do one of his household chores for him while he is working or at a practice. Trust me, he will appreciate the time and effort you took to make his life easier.

Lastly, learn to show your partner love by spending time with him. I know this may be hard to believe, but you two can spend time together, have fun together, and do something other than sex. Go to the park together. Go to a concert, game, movie, or show together. Let him pick the activity, and you organize it. He will have a blast.

By learning to show love in ways other than giving your body, you will make your partner happy and develop essential love skills that will help you become a great wife one day.

Emotional power of sex

Men and women are different in many ways. Physiologically, obviously, but also psychologically. The difference in the way males and females think is also a reflection of their differences in feelings.

In general, women tend to think a bit more emotionally than their counterparts. This only makes sense, thinking back to our natural motherly instincts to love, care, and nurture others. However, what we sometimes don't realize when we are young is that sex for us isn't just physical; it has great emotional power. Sex is the most intimate act you can perform with someone. It is truly a giving of your body to another individual. The emotional connection you will feel with someone through sexual intimacy is one that cannot be explained in words; it can only be felt. And it is meant to be felt after you are married to that special individual who will be lucky enough one day to call himself your husband.

The emotional power of intimacy is a beautiful thing when the right time comes. However, in your teenage years, these emotions can become like a prison cell. You cannot escape the feelings. They surround you like steel-barred cells. When things do not work out with your partner, you are left feeling completely devastated. You feel embarrassed, used, and dirty. And this emotional impact is one it can be hard ever to escape.

Your body is sacred, girls. Treat it that way. Save it for yourself. Save it for your future husband, to give him the ultimate gift of purity.

Make your husband proud

By spending your time during your teenage years focusing on learning to show love in ways other than sex, you are already practicing how to be a wonderful wife. Your words and actions will one day make a man extremely happy and proud to be your husband. As much as men will put up a macho "I take care of my woman" attitude, at the end of the day they all enjoy being cared for or catered toward. In addition to being appreciative and proud of the way you show love, they will be even more proud to be the husband of a woman who respected herself so much for so many years. They'll be proud to say that their wife treated her body like the sacred chamber it truly was and saved herself. They'll be beyond proud that they got to say "I do" to a woman who was beautiful inside and out, to a woman fueled by strength and self-respect.

That is why purity is the ultimate wedding gift you can give your husband one day.

Some of you may be thinking, *It is too late for me to give the gift of purity to my future husband.* But just because you have given yourself away before does not mean you can't make the decision now to protect your body and your heart. You know what your values are. We all get off the path in various ways throughout our lives. The detours are not what define us as women. The strength we have deep within us to make the choice to get back on track is what establishes who we truly are.

Everlasting consequences

If the beauty of saving yourself for intimacy with your husband one day does not get your attention, then I hope the reality of consequences does. With every decision you make comes a consequence. Sometimes it is a positive consequence; at other times, not so much. For example, with the decision to have sex as a teenager, you immediately run the risk of pregnancy or STDs. Even if you are on birth control, there is still a risk of both. Pregnancy and STDs are the immediate potential consequences.

However, what many of us do not realize at an early age is the long-term consequences that can result from teenage sexual intercourse. For example, according to the CDC, untreated STDs cause infertility in at least 24,000 American women each year. What does infertility mean? Infertility means an inability to get pregnant. Just imagine having to tell your husband one day that you can't get pregnant because of a decision you made when you were 18. Just because you are "on birth control" or "practice safe sex" does not mean there are not everlasting consequences to the decisions you are making as a teenager. Think long and hard about who you are, what you stand for, and who you want to be one day. Choose to do right for yourself, your future husband, and most importantly, your future children.

Summary

- You can show love toward a guy through ways other than sex.
- Your emotional attachment to someone drastically increases once intercourse has occurred.
- A man finds beauty in a woman who can show love and care in ways other than sex.
- Lasting consequences of teenage sex can include pregnancy, STDs, and infertility.

family

"Other things may change us, but we start and end with the family."

—Anthony Brandt

I know what many of you thought when you flipped the page and saw the title for this chapter: *Family . . . I can't stand mine! For sure I'm not reading this chapter. Next!* I know exactly where you're coming from. I thought the same thing from about ages 14 to 19.

I come from a very close-knit family. We're one of those families that calls one another 15 times a day and tells one another everything. We're all up in one another's business 24-7. Growing up, I lived with my mother, father, and sister Danielle. My father owned his own construction company, and my mother helped manage the company and raised my sister and me. I was lucky enough to be raised in a home with two loving parents who were both very much involved in my life. My parents were extremely hardworking, so they had the financial means to provide an above-average standard of living for my sister and me. As an adolescent, I did not recognize how fortunate I was to have this kind of upbringing. I truly wish that, when I was a teenager, someone had helped open my eyes to how important family is. That's why I'm including this chapter now.

Yes, of course you've heard a thousand times from your parents, "You'd better start loving us: we are the only people who will always be here for you!" Or your teachers may tell you right before Thanksgiving break, "Make sure you tell your family how much you love them and how thankful you are for them." However, no one truly dives into the depth and importance of family when you are in your teenage years. It is my hope that I can not only explain the impact your family has on your life during your teenage years but soften your heart and open your eyes to the idea that you might actually *like* them.

Scary thought, I know. Stick with me here.

Through my research and interviews, I've come to realize family influences the life of a teenage girl through three main avenues:

- Building the foundation of her identity
- Showing her the basis of love
- Teaching her that blood is thicker than water

Building the foundation of her identity

Identity is the distinguishing personality or character of an individual. Personality is a set of emotional qualities that helps the person present themselves and communicate to others. For example, some people have an outgoing personality, while others are more introverted. A bit of your personality is genetic, but your personality and character are strongly based on your environment. So where do our morals come from? What environment teaches us to value what we value? How do we learn to behave the way we do? It all comes down to one common denominator: family.

In our infancy, we are helpless. We cannot even do the simple tasks that require zero thought from us today, such as eating and using the restroom on our own. We must rely on our parents or other family members to feed us, change our diapers, and generally sustain life. As we enter the toddler stage, we rely on our parents to protect us from the dangers our curious minds can get us into. We want to run toward every pool of water and jump in, even though we can't swim. We want to touch the hot stove, just because Mom said not to. We want to play basketball in the street, because we haven't played out there before. The curiosity of toddlers is what helps them learn, experience, and grow. However, this curiosity must be monitored and guided in a safe direction by parents, or else no toddler would ever survive.

Whether you want to admit it or not, no matter how much you may think you hate your parents at this very moment, they are the only reason you are here. Your parents have helped provide for you physically, mentally, emotionally, and financially through your entire life. As a kid, you cannot provide a home for yourself yet. Some of you may not even be able to drive yet. And as much as you think you have all the answers in the world, there are many things you still need your parents' guidance on. (Taxes, for instance. Just wait until the day you have to do your own taxes for the first time. You'll be calling home to Momma for some help!)

Not only have your parents been your providers for survival through the years, they have shaped you into who you are today. Your personality and character are byproducts of the environment in which you have been raised. Your family has instilled certain values and beliefs into your mind that guide the decisions you make daily. You have not just naturally treated people with respect and kindness; you were taught this through your upbringing. When you offer to help someone in need, you do so because your parents have taught you to help others. When you decide not to get into a car with a driver who has been drinking, it's because your parents have told you thousands of times the risks of this behavior.

At the end of the day, your character is strongly molded by the influence of your family.

Showing her the basis of love

You have already received and expressed love in many different ways. You have felt love from family, friends, teachers, coaches, pastors, maybe a significant other. However, one form of love many of you have not realized you have received is the *unconditional* love of your family.

Unconditional love is love without limitations. No matter how good or bad things may be, the love is still there. Families provide unconditional love to us every day. No matter how much wrong we have done, how many lies we have told, how many hearts we have broken, every night when we lay our head on the pillow, our family still loves us.

As a teenager, I did not understand unconditional love. It was not until I was about 22 and in a relationship with someone who was a wonderful person, but just not the right fit for me, that I began to understand. This relationship had been going on for six years. We were high school sweethearts who stayed together all the way through college. I was fresh out of school and working in the volleyball industry, which had been my life's passion. Everything in my life was going perfectly—great job, awesome friends—but my boyfriend and I were just not meshing. Unfortunately, during this time, I made some horrible decisions that hurt a lot of people. Tears were shed, trust was broken, and hearts were shattered.

However, one thing that remained constant throughout all of this pain was the unconditional love I received from my family. While they did not approve of my actions, they still loved me. No matter how many sins I committed and no matter how much I hurt them, their love was still there. There is no more humbling experience than to be on your hands and knees, broken, scared, and helpless, and still to feel the unconditional love of your parents, still wanting to hold you, no matter how much wrong you may have done.

Girls, a few friends will betray you. You may fall in and out of love with different partners. Teachers and coaches will come and go. However, the love of a mother and father is something you will get to take with you to your grave.

The second foundation of love your family provides to you is an example of love within a marriage and family setting. Some of you may be raised in a family of two parents who are married and raising the family under one roof. Some of you may have parents who are divorced, and you spend weekdays at Mom's and weekends at Dad's. Some of you may have a house with a mother, stepfather, and family in one neighborhood and a house with a father, stepmother, and family in another neighborhood. Every family tree looks a little different. However, one thing they all have in common is that they influence your expectations of love.

The way you have witnessed your parents, stepparents, and other family members interacting within romantic relationships has painted a picture of intimate love in your mind. Maybe what you have witnessed is something you hope for one day in your own marriage. You might want to emulate the ways your mother has loved and cared for your father. Maybe you have watched certain behaviors and characteristics and thought that you did not want to treat your future husband in any of those ways, or that you did not want your husband to treat you in those ways. Or maybe you have witnessed broken marriages where love has died and tears are shed, and you want that never to happen to you.

Teaching her that blood is thicker than water

Right now you are in a stage in your life where you feel family is your biggest enemy. Your parents constantly want to butt into your social life, your little brother is the most annoying creature on the planet, and if your mother tells you one more time to go visit your grandma, you are going to run your head into a wall. I understand you did not pick these people to be your family. Right now, you would rather chill with your girlfriends and binge-watch Netflix until two in the morning, or Snapchat with your boyfriend. Anything but spending time with your family. I remember thinking the same thing. As teenage girls, we struggle just to get by from Sunday to Thursday so that we can make it to Friday night football games and Saturday night parties. Brad Paisley said it best when he sang, "At 17, it's hard to see past Friday night." It couldn't be more true.

However, at 28, I look back on my high school career and I am only able to rummage up one or two memories from the football games and parties I went to. These experiences, while they seem so big to you right now, truly are so small. They are not what you will truly remember from your high school years. It is the friendships and relationships built during this time that will stick with you.

The night I graduated high school, my parents allowed me to have a "kid party" after my family party came to an end. I was so excited. Everyone in school had been talking about it for the past month. As my family party was going on, I was buzzing around talking to aunts, uncles, cousins, and grandparents. I was being polite, smiling, and thanking people for coming to my party. However, in the back of my mind, all I could think about was getting this family party over with so that all my friends could get there. My graduation "kid" party resulted in about

200 teenagers in a field on my parents' farm. At that moment, I thought it was the highlight of my life.

On my wedding day, as I stood next to my husband and looked out into the church, I actually thought back to that graduation party. I thought of it because, out of the 200 teenagers who were at my party that evening, only four of them remained in my life ten years later to attend my wedding. Those four were the bridesmaids standing by my side. However, as I scanned the crowd, every family member who had attended that graduation party was sitting in the pews before me, watching me marry the man of my dreams.

It was at this moment that I truly understood the value of the phrase "blood is thicker than water." Throughout your life, many people will come and go. Some will leave pieces of themselves in your heart forever. Some will betray you, break you, and hurt you. Some will have no significant impact or value to you at all. Each person will touch you in a different way, leave a different mark. As these people come and go, you will take what they leave with you and let it strengthen you. But while the seasons of friends and acquaintances constantly change, you can always count on family never to fade.

Blood is thicker than water. You have been raised in this world through the unconditional love of your parents, and one day—hopefully years down the road, after you have lived out your purpose on this Earth—you will be laid to rest with the loving family *you* have created standing around you. The love of family is full circle. Embrace it.

55

Summary

Your family shapes you in three ways:

They build the foundation of your identity.
- They teach you values, morals, and beliefs.
- They create the environment you are raised in, which influences your behaviors.

They show you the basis of love.
- They are the first individuals to show you what unconditional love is.
- Their relationship is the first romantic relationship you are introduced to.

They teach you that blood is thicker than water.
- People will come and go throughout your life, but family is forever tied to you.
- The smiles, laughter, and tears shared throughout the years with family are what create the everlasting bond strengthened through the blood of family.

Part Two

Your Dreams

CHAPTER EIGHT

Passion. Purpose. Power.

∽♡∽

"If you organize your life around your passion, you can turn your passion into your story and then turn your story into something bigger—something that matters."

—Blake Mycoskie

From a very early age, I was a passionate person in all that I did, from showing love to my family to doing well in school to playing the game I loved most, volleyball. My passion toward life was fueled by my energetic spirit, loving heart, and gritty work ethic. Growing up, I was far from the most intelligent kid in the classroom. I was terrible at math, and I couldn't spell to save my life. If I'm being truthful, to this day I struggle with both. I was also not the most athletic kid in my class.

As a child, I knew that I did not have extraordinary God-given academic or athletic talents. However, as I compared myself to my peers, I realized I had something over all of them: *passion*.

If you are an individual who often feels frustrated or irritated, who would rather sleep until noon than get up in the morning, or who feels as if she rarely gets anything accomplished throughout the day, then I'm begging you to focus now more than ever. If I am only able to teach you one lesson with this book, I want this to be it. If you are able to grasp the information that lies ahead and apply it to your life, I have no doubt the other aspects of your life will follow suit.

Have you ever wondered how the class president seems to have everything in her life organized perfectly as she carries herself confidently through the halls? Or how the captain of the varsity basketball team keeps straight A's, practices daily, works out every morning before school, has all the popular friends, and still has enough energy to smile at you every day? The answer is that they have found their passion, their purpose. They have found their "why" in life.

Each of us is unique. We have been given different gifts. We have different callings, different purposes we are supposed to live out during our time here on Earth. The sad reality, however, is that many individuals do not have the persistence to find their calling, the work ethic to rise to their calling, or the discipline to live out their calling.

You have been given special gifts. You have a purpose on this Earth. You have a calling you are expected to rise to. You have an extremely bright future ahead of you. You may not know what that calling is yet, and that is okay. I did not know either in my adolescent years. However, I knew I was passionate.

Passion is the only thing you need to get you started on your quest for your "why" in life. When you have passion in your soul, it fuels you to achieve things that may not seem humanly possible.

Passion keeps you focused on the task at hand. Passion makes the long, grueling hours of work you put into something seem as if they were never work to begin with. Passion makes you proud of who you are and what you show to the world.

Think to yourself, right now: What are you passionate about? What do you love to do? What would you do all the time if you were allowed to? What would you love to do for the rest of your life, if it could be turned into a career? Are you passionate about a specific hobby, like music or photography? Are you passionate about helping others?

If you are sitting there thinking, *I'm not passionate about anything*, then try doing something different in your life. Try a new club or sport. Meet a new friend and see what they are interested in. Continue to search for your passion until you find something.

I am being stern with you on this topic because I can promise you that without passion burning inside your soul, you are traveling down a lonely, miserable path. I have seen it happen too many times: talented people letting their skills go to waste because they can't identify what their passions truly are. They spend every day just going through the motions, hardly getting by, being miserable with their lives and causing misery to all those around them as well.

I want you to take a moment and list below three passions you have. If you can't think of what you are passionate about at this time, continue to explore until you can come back to this page and record your passions.

1.

2.

3.

When you are passionate about something, it excites you. It becomes a part of who you are. It makes you want to get up every morning to your alarm clock and continue to work on the passion and share it with others.

Most importantly, if you are passionate about something, it gives you *purpose*. It gives you clarity on what is important to you in life, a vision for what you want to achieve and what you want your life to look like. The incredible thing about having purpose is that you feel alive. A ton of research has been done on this topic, and it shows that individuals who feel they have a purpose in life produce higher levels of work, live more active and healthy lifestyles, and feel more happiness within their relationships. As you can see, when you find your purpose, the odds are in your favor that you are going to experience more joy.

I'm sure you are sitting there thinking to yourself, *I'm just a teenager!*

How am I supposed to know what my purpose is right now? I can't even drive myself anywhere yet. I understand your point. However, you are never too young to think about your purpose and start cultivating the mindset necessary to be passionate and live it out.

Part of finding your purpose and living it out is constantly reflecting on and evaluating who you are. Many people struggle to do these things, but the most successful people in the world have it mastered. If you were to ask any professional athlete, business leader, or world leader if they practiced self-reflection, you would find that they all do. Without reflection and evaluation of oneself, there is no way to track progress.

Many people run away from self-evaluation due to their own lack of confidence. They feel as if all they have to look at are their failures, and it breaks them down. Others avoid self-reflection because, deep down, they know they are not living the lives they truly want. They are ashamed and embarrassed by their lives. It is easier for them to ignore the thoughts and just keep going through the motions of the day than to accept this shame. Unfortunately, these people look at self-evaluation similarly to how they look at life itself: half empty.

Instead, I challenge you to look at self-reflection and evaluation as a chance to look at your life as being half full. With every moment of self-reflection, you are taking the opportunity to look at the things you do well in your life but also at the things you could improve on to add value and happiness to your life. These failures or weaknesses you think you have are simply opportunities for you to learn something new, try something different, and better yourself.

A person's mindset is what separates him or her from the underperforming. Those who can see the depth, beauty, and power of self-reflection are those who will approach it with the right mindset. Try to see self-reflection as a positive opportunity, not a list of negative failures. I challenge you to take this time to write down three strengths you think you have and three weaknesses you think you have.

Three Strengths

1.

2.

3.

Three Weaknesses

1.

2.

3.

Now ask yourself: Are any of these strengths tied to the passions you listed previously in this chapter? Do these strengths allow you to do things you enjoy? Do these strengths provide you with success as a person, student, athlete, or artist? Do you do things daily that bring out these strengths in your work and actions? Chances are, if you were truthful about your strengths, you are starting to be able to paint a picture in your mind of what your purpose truly is.

Now, you might not know the full depth of this purpose yet. You may not know where you are supposed to go with it or what the next steps are. Don't panic. I didn't either. Like I told you before, from a very early age, all I knew about my life was that I was a passionate person. I also knew from around the age of 12 that I wanted to do nothing more than play volleyball. It was all I could think about or talk about. Heck, I even dreamed about it often. However, I could not see past anything but the surface-level concept that I loved volleyball. End of story.

Some of you might be in the same place I was at your age. You know you are passionate about something, but you don't know what your purpose is. That's okay. Keep doing what you're doing. Keep being passionate. Keep showing up every day and giving 100% to whatever it is you do and to the people around you. Continue to bring energy and joy to what you do. If you can continue doing that, you have already begun building your purpose in life.

Imagine your purpose in life being like a house. By continuing to be passionate about what you are doing now, you are pouring the basement or foundation of a house. You are creating a positive mindset. You are establishing skills and traits that are going to help you be successful, not only in what you are pursuing now, but in many different dreams and aspirations you will pursue throughout your life. These dreams and aspirations are like the walls of the house. They begin to shape what the house will actually look like, and they provide structure and stability. Without the foundation— the skills and mindset you are creating now in your adolescent years—the walls cannot be built. And, just like in building a house, your purpose in life takes time to figure out, to develop, and to live out.

Now look back to your weaknesses. Are these weaknesses correlated with a fear you have? Are these weaknesses holding you back from doing something great or being the woman you have always wanted to be? Do these weaknesses prevent you from moving forward in a positive manner? If you can truly be honest with yourself on these answers, you have already taken the next step necessary in finding your purpose. Identifying what you're passionate about and then reflecting on your strengths and weaknesses will help you find your purpose, through which you will gain happiness and influence others in a powerful and positive way.

Think back to the image of the house. Its foundation is your passion, and its walls are your purpose. Now for the final touch that makes the house complete: *power*. Once you have established your passion and learned how that passion impacts your purpose or calling, you then have the power to live it out and share it with others. Many people never make it to this final stage of true power.

I want to be very clear that the term "power," as I'm using it here, should not be seen as an authority you have been given over others. Many of you have probably heard the common phrase "with great power comes great responsibility." I could not stress the immense truth of this quote more. If you identify what your passion is and allow it to drive your purpose in life, you will open many roads for yourself. With many roads come many paths, and with many paths come many choices. It is my hope that you choose to let your passion and purpose energize you from the inside out in a positive way and that you share your gifts with the world through your calling. It is my hope that your passion and purpose make you feel strong and confident, giving you the courage to serve and share with others. It is my hope that you reach this level of power as a woman and that you choose to do right with it.

Like I mentioned before, at your age I had no idea what my purpose in life was. I also never even dreamed that I would have the power to help influence others in a positive way. However, I always knew that my passion was volleyball, so I continued to pursue that passion in any way I could. I played the game for hours, on any team I could make. When I was old enough to work at volleyball camps, I turned my passion into financial income that allowed me to go out with my friends on the weekends. I pursued a collegiate volleyball career, which helped pay for my education. Then I found a way to support myself through volleyball as a full-time job.

Through each of these different milestones, my passion remained the same. However, throughout this journey, my purpose became clearer to me. My purpose has always been to help lead and serve others. At a young age, I was living this purpose by helping classmates and teammates. As a volleyball coach, my purpose is to help athletes grow on and off the floor into strong, hardworking, confident young women. As a volleyball director, my purpose is to help lead fellow coaches so they can influence athletes in a positive way. As a writer, my purpose is to help inspire, guide, and empower you to become the best version of yourself.

I share this with you to help you understand that we don't always know what our purposes are. However, if we know what we are passionate about, through time and commitment to those passions, our purposes will begin to unfold. Your purpose will begin to become clearer with time, just like mine did. As your purpose becomes clearer to you, allow your passion to fuel you, and be persistent. You will find the inner strength and courage to live out your purpose in a powerful and positive way.

When it comes to the definition of success, everyone has a different answer. Some people define success by money, accolades, or friends and/or social media followers. However, I believe that true success is when you can wake up in the morning, look at yourself with a smile, and say, "I have a true passion. I have a purpose in life. I have the courage and power to serve others in a positive way." When you can do that, you are truly living. You have reached success, and I can guarantee you that along with success will come great happiness.

Do not wait. Start now. Find your passion. Make it your life's purpose. Most importantly, have the courage to live it out and influence others in a powerful way.

Summary

- Find your passion in life, make it your life's purpose, and live it out to influence others in a positive way.
- Self-reflection is about understanding your strengths and weaknesses, not about degrading yourself for your so-called failures.
- The only failure in life is to look at what went wrong as a failure instead of as an opportunity for growth.
- Mastering self-reflection, identifying your strengths and weaknesses, and learning to grow from mistakes is the recipe for a lifetime of happiness.

CHAPTER NINE

Goal-Setting

∽♡∽

"Goals. There's no telling what you can do when you get inspired by them. There's no telling what you can do when you believe in them. And there's no telling what will happen when you act upon them."

—Jim Rohn

Previously, we discussed how having a passion will fuel your body with energy and lead you to your purpose in life. However, without a clear vision and plan of how to live those things out, you will unfortunately achieve nothing. Approaching your life with no vision or plan is like going on a road trip without putting an address into Google Maps. You are going to drive around aimlessly, never making it to your desired destination. So if you want to make it to that beautiful beach with the sun setting along the horizon, buckle up, and let's take a ride through goal-setting.

Each of you has heard your parents, teachers, instructors, and coaches say, "You have to set goals for yourself." You think to yourself, *Blah, Blah, Blah. Yeah, I get it. Next!* If you are sick and tired of people telling you to set goals, then hang with me here for a second. I think I can help alleviate some of this frustration for you. I want to help you see goal-setting in a different light than what you have ever been taught before.

Oftentimes, people will try to influence what your goals "should" be. That is the first issue. Your goals must be just that: *yours*. They must be based on the clarity of your own mind. What you want to achieve. What you want your life to look like one year, five years, ten years, twenty years down the road.

When referring to clarity, I mean the vision you have for your life. Having clarity and vision for who you are and what you want your life to look like takes great self-reflection. You must constantly ask yourself questions such as: *Who am I? What do I value? What do I enjoy doing? Who in my life adds positive value? Who in my life brings toxic energy? What are my strengths? What are my weaknesses?* These are just a few of the questions people who have a clear vision for their lives ask themselves on a daily basis. People with clarity have curious minds. They often research and ask questions until they find the answers they need.

If you want to be one of those people who actually creates their life vision into reality, you can't just think about it. You must set goals. Then you must take action to achieve these goals. Honestly, taking action isn't the most difficult part. Planning the action steps in order to achieve the goal is the step most people never achieve. This is the hardest part. Once you get past it, you are going to be just fine.

What do I mean by action steps? Action steps are like the driving directions Siri shouts at you from your phone. These are the steps you must take in order to achieve your goals. So, what do they look like? How do we create them? First, we must break down each goal piece by piece.

The number one error many of us make when setting goals is in setting unclear goals. When setting a goal, remember that if you are missing any foundational pieces of the goal, you will never be able to follow through. Why? It is simple: There is no direction. No plan. No deadline. No urgency.

When creating your goals, make sure to focus on including all key components. To help you understand what I mean, I have created the chart below. This chart includes the four key components of a goal. I believe these guidelines are needed in order to make sure your goals are designed in the most opportune way for you to achieve them.

Four Key Components of a Goal

Specific

- State your goal.
- Include who, what, where, when, and why.
- Example: I want to make my upper body stronger, so my current goal is to be able to do 10 push-ups three weeks from today.

Measurable

- Involve specific numbers when you can.
- Example: As above, specifying the number of push-ups.
- A measurable goal allows you to track progress.

Attainable

- Ten is a reasonable number of push-ups for a beginner to build up to within three weeks.
- Make your goal reasonable for you.
- Be careful not to set goals that are too easy. An attainable goal should still be a challenge to work toward.

Time-Bound

- Set a time frame for accomplishing your goal.
- A deadline helps you stay motivated and on track.
- Example: The goal above specifically says you want to meet the challenge by the end of the next three weeks.

Now for more information about each component. For the purpose of helping you understand the four components of goal-setting, I will use the same "goal example" used in the chart.

Specific. This is key. You must be very *specific* in regard to what your goal is. The goal is, "I want to make my upper body stronger, so my current goal is to be able to do 10 push-ups three weeks from today." This goal is very clear as to what I am trying to achieve.

Measurable. This is one many people leave out when setting their goals. Making a goal *measurable* means you can track your progress. It usually involves numbers. Referencing back to our goal example, I was very clear that I wanted to achieve *10* push-ups. I included a number so that I could track my success over time. Tying a number to your goal helps keep you focused and dialed in on achieving it. It also allows you to feel great success when you do finally achieve it. What many people do not realize is that achieving and celebrating a goal fuels your soul to want to set and achieve more goals. In the long run, this will increase your productivity and success overall.

Attainable. This means the goal is reasonable *for you*. It is not completely out of your reach. It is neither too hard nor too easy. For example, if you can already do nine push-ups, this goal would not meet the criterion of "attainable" for you. It is too easy. On the flip side, setting the goal at 100 push-ups within three weeks would not be attainable for a beginner; you'd be setting yourself up for failure (and possibly for injury).

I'm not saying being able to do 100 push-ups can't be your long-term goal. That is fine. Just make sure you give yourself an attainable time frame to achieve the goal. Not too hard. Not too easy. Just challenging enough to push you to be the best version of yourself.

Keep in mind that a larger goal can be reached by setting smaller, attainable goals. This will help you stay on track and see the progress you are making. For example, "I want to be a doctor by the end of the year" is not attainable if you're starting from the beginning. You must have years and years of education, internship, and residency under your belt in order to be a doctor. Setting an attainable goal, such as taking your medical school admittance test by a certain date and scoring well on it, would be a better start.

Time-bound. Time is the final factor to goal-setting, and if you forget it, chances are you will never complete your goal. Being *time-bound* refers to setting a deadline on achieving the goal. Referencing back to the example we have used: I want to do 10 push-ups by the end of *three weeks*. Research shows that if a person has a deadline such as this one, they stay more focused and have more urgency to finish the task at hand.

Think about it. If you are given a homework assignment that is due tomorrow, chances are you are going to do it tonight before you go to sleep so that it is ready for class tomorrow. However, if a teacher gives you the same assignment and tells you the test will have problems similar to these, but she does not tell you to complete them and turn them in the next day, chances are you will put them in your binder and never look at them again. Why? Because there was no deadline given to you to complete those problems. With no deadline, you subconsciously think you have no reason or urgency to complete them.

The goals you set for your life are the same way. If you set goals that have very definite, time-bound deadlines, you will drastically increase your chances of achieving them when compared to goals with no deadlines.

Short-term versus long-term goals

When thinking about your goals in life, it is important to understand a couple of things. First, you want to realize you need goals for all parts of your life. Think of your life like an entire pizza, and view every slice as a different "piece" of your life. These pieces could be school, sports, theatre, music, family, and friends, just to name a few. It is important for you to understand that each of these different pieces of your life requires you to set goals within that area.

It is also important to understand there is a distinct difference between *short-term* and *long-term* goals. While the definite timing of short- versus long-term is a little different for everyone, generally short-term goals are ones you plan to complete within the next year, while long-term goals are two to five, or five to ten, or ten-plus years down the road.

Think back to the *specific, measurable, attainable,* and *time-bound* foundational pieces of goal-setting. Now flip to the last page of the book and look at the Goal-Setting Worksheet provided there. I challenge you to take some time right now. Do not read on. Stop. Grab a pen or pencil, go to the end of the book, and begin to fill out the sheet.

If you are reading this sentence, then you completed the Goal-Setting Worksheet. Now you have a better vision of what your goals are, both in the near future and years down the road. If you thought back to what we learned in regard to the four foundational components of goal-setting, then you have a very clear goal ahead of you.

However, now you need *action steps* to help you climb the ladder of success. How do you create these?

Goal-setting action steps:

Step 1: Set the goal

Step 2: Share the goal

Step 3: Set the mini-goals

Step 4: Give a timeline to the mini-goals

Step 5: Find people who can help

Step 6: Celebrate the mini-wins

Step 1: Set the goal

Guess what? Good news, guys! You've already completed this part! Easy step. You have already created your specific, measurable, attainable, and time-bound goal. Just make sure you have written it down. Put it somewhere you will constantly see it. You want it to remind you every day why and how you are doing what you are doing.

If you truly want to achieve your goals, you want them to be like a little voice in your brain that never goes away, constantly reminding you of what you want and why you are working so hard to achieve it.

Step 2: Share the goal

Sharing your goal with others will be monumental in keeping you on the right track toward achievement of the goal. When you share your goal with others, it immediately requires accountability from you. It will fuel you to work harder toward achieving the goal, simply because you will not want to admit to these people that you have not progressed toward your goal. It will keep you from getting lazy or quitting.

Step 3: Set the mini-goals

Setting mini-goals is the part many people find most difficult. So, not surprisingly, this is the step many people do not complete, and that results in the goal never being achieved. Mini-goals are the steps needed in order to move you closer to achieving your goal. For example, when I set a goal to write and publish this book, I had to define very clear mini-goals:

- Research topics and interview people whose wisdom I want to share
- Write each chapter
- Find a literary agent to represent the book
- Get a publisher
- Market the book in order for people like you to purchase it

Each of these mini-goals brought me one step closer to finishing my goal and getting it into the hands of readers like you.

Step 4: Give a timeline to the mini-goals

After you determine what mini-goals will help you move closer to success, set a timeline for each. Remember, without a timeline, there is no deadline to the goal. Without a deadline, there is no urgency. Without urgency, the goal is never achieved.

Step 5: find people who can help

Success is never achieved alone. Someone is always there along the way to help you climb the ladder of success. Embrace this and use it to your advantage. Think back to your goal and list three people who have achieved this goal before you. Research them. Study their achievements. Reach out to them. Ask for their help. Learn from them.

Trust me when I tell you that most people want to help you develop. They want to help you succeed. Yes, of course there will be some people who won't give you the time of day, but I promise you that the good leaders—the ones you truly want to learn from and be like—will help you. Go find them. Allow them to help you climb the ladder of success.

Step 6: Celebrate the mini-wins

Oftentimes, we never complete this step. As humans, we are naturally hard on ourselves and belittle our own achievements. We don't see accomplishing the "mini-wins" as a point of achievement or a reason to celebrate. However, this is where people go so wrong. If you never celebrate the little accomplishments you make in life, you will begin to lose your desire to achieve the larger ones. Without celebrating the mini-triumphs, you will find your energy begins to fade, your mindset becomes foggy, and your desires start to seem vague. If you truly want to achieve major goals you have set for yourself, both short-term and long-term, you must begin to celebrate the mini-wins, even if that means celebrating doing your very first push-up! By celebrating these, you will keep your energy alive and keep your mind on the ultimate goal, and your desire for success will remain bright.

It takes focus and discipline to truly put in the time, thought, and planning to achieve goals. If you can make a habit of this at an early age, you are setting yourself up for success and happiness in all parts of your life for years to come.

While the steps I have provided in this chapter are designed to help turn your goals into reality, it is important to realize that achieving a goal is never guaranteed. Sometimes, no matter how perfectly you design a goal or how clear your action steps are, you fail. That is the reality of life. Sometimes you win and sometimes you lose. However, with every failure, there is something to be gained: knowledge.

The power of knowledge is immeasurable. If you are able to look at a shortcoming with the mindset of learning a new lesson, then you have succeeded. Maybe this was not the success you had originally wanted, but you have succeeded. I promise. Learning a lesson from a failure is monumental in your personal development. Having learned the lesson, you will make a different move the next time around, and chances are you will then achieve that goal. Nelson Mandela said it best: "I never lose. I either win or learn."

You have all the tools you need to chase your dreams, so go! Dream big. Set goals. Take action. When you win, celebrate. When you fail, learn. Follow this path, and you will never lose.

Summary

Four key components of a goal:
- Specific
- Measurable
- Attainable
- Time-Bound

Goal-setting action steps:
Step 1: Set the goal
Step 2: Share the goal
Step 3: Set the mini-goals
Step 4: Give a timeline to the mini-goals
Step 5: Find people who can help
Step 6: Celebrate the mini-wins

CHAPTER TEN

Circle of Influence

∽♡∼

"Remove negative people from your life. The people you spend time with influence your attitude, thoughts, and success more than you think."

—**Author unknown**

Every day, you interact with different people, doing different activities, in different environments. Although we do not always realize it, each of these people, activities, and places indirectly and directly influences who we are. I like to say these interactions make up one's *circle of influence.* Your circle of influence will constantly evolve throughout your life. However, while the people, activities, and places within the circle of influence will change, one thing will remain consistent: the circle's effect on you.

Your circle of influence plays a huge role in your attitude, thoughts, and decision-making. It shapes the person you are, the morals you stand by, the decisions you make, and ultimately the success you have as a woman. For this reason, you must be extremely careful whom you allow in, what activities you allow yourself to be involved with, and what environments you allow yourself to be immersed in.

Choose wisely whom you allow into your life. If you have negative, drama-filled, toxic people in your life, their mindsets, attitudes, and behaviors will begin to rub off on you. Their negativity will drag you down and transform your mind into that of a pessimist. Their drama will begin to consume your brain, resulting in an angry and bitter heart. Their toxicity will turn you toxic. Before you know it, you will have become a person you don't even recognize anymore, a person whom, quite frankly, you hate.

Think about the people in your life at this time: family, friends, peers, teammates, teachers, coaches, mentors, anyone you interact with on any level. Ask yourself the following questions: Are they positive people? Do they share similar morals to mine? Are their behaviors and decision-making in line with my values? Do they bring positive energy to my life? Do they help influence me to be a better version of myself every day? If you cannot answer yes to all of these questions in a given relationship, reevaluate that relationship immediately.

Research has shown that you are a direct reflection of the five people you spend the most time with. With that in mind, be very selective about sharing your time with people. Many of you have probably heard the phrase "guilty by association"; unfortunately, this is not a fallacy. Consider your friendships. Even if you have different morals than your friends, participate in different activities than they do, or make different social decisions than they do, you will be considered by many to be the same as they are due to your association with them. I share this with you to help you think twice about your current friendships. Ask yourself: *Am I okay with how my peers, adults, and society as a whole view my friends?* Because, ultimately, how they see your friends is how they probably see you. For example, chances are that if your friends drink and smoke, people will think you do as well, whether they see you doing so or not. Make sure you are satisfied with the image being given off by your friends. If you are not, then it is time you make the very difficult decision to remove them from your life.

Cutting people out who do not bring positive energy, values, and worth to your life also helps bring you more to life than ever. As we discussed earlier in this chapter, your circle of influence plays a key role in your attitudes, thoughts, and decision-making. By removing negative people and surrounding yourself with highly energetic, hardworking, caring people, you'll be on the path to becoming successful, but most importantly, you'll become a genuinely happy woman.

While the people you interact with on a daily basis play a major role in your circle of influence and who you are, they are not the only ones. In order to take your success and happiness to another level, you must first realize you cannot do it alone. You need people that I like to call *advancers*.

Advancers are individuals who are older, wiser, and more successful than you. Oftentimes, teenagers think they are invincible and that they know it all; they don't want anyone's help. I was the same way. Now when I think back to this phase of my life I laugh, knowing how young and dumb I truly was. Some young people do realize they don't know everything, but they can't see when someone is right in front of them and ready to offer wisdom. I can help you with that.

Knowing that you have much to learn about life itself is the first step in advancing yourself. Next, you need to decide who can help you get to where you want to go. This is where the advancers come into play. The reality is, there are always people around you who are smarter, more experienced, and more successful than you are. Do not let that intimidate you. Instead, let it excite you! Choose to interact with those people, and use the interactions as an opportunity to grow.

You may be asking yourself, *Who could my advancers be?* You can find advancers in all walks of your life. One might be your best friend's parent, who works in an industry that interests you as a future career. One might be your boss, whose leadership you've always been impressed by. One might be a youth minister at your church whom you have always admired for their caring spirit. Whoever your advancers may be, find ways to interact with them more. Ask them questions. Discuss current events with them. Ask to work for them. Do anything you can to be around them. Through these interactions, they give you knowledge and wisdom that far exceed what you can learn from a textbook. They will pass down to you the power of experience, and there is no price tag on that information.

Your immediate thought is probably, *That sounds great, but why would any successful adult want to give me the time of day?* Trust me when I tell you: They want to help you, teach you, and guide you. They want to help influence you to be the strongest version of yourself. Why do they want to do these things? Because someone did it for them, and now they are passing the torch, just as you will one day do for someone you mentor. Also, people love to talk about their own lives and how they got to where they are. They get excited to share their stories. The advancers you come into contact with throughout your life will feel the same way. They enjoy sharing their lives with an eager young mind, so let them, and be grateful for them. Without them, you wouldn't achieve success.

One thing you can lose sight of when you begin to seek wisdom from others is the act of gratitude. You can start to become so eager to advance to different levels in your life that all you can see is the success you achieve. With each milestone you reach, you become more prideful and greedy. This is a dangerous trap to fall into. Never forget your roots. Never forget where you started and all the people who helped you along the way. Like I've said before, you achieve nothing alone. Someone or something *always* helps you achieve your goal. Don't let your ego blind you. Remember always to give thanks to those who helped you along the way to success.

One of the most touching ways to show appreciation is through a handwritten thank-you card. This is a lost art in today's society, especially with the younger generation. So many people today simply want to shoot someone a thank-you text. That is a surface-level, convenient for you, thoughtless way of showing appreciation. It takes zero effort. However, the everlasting impact of thoughtfulness, love, and care that a handwritten thank-you card leaves is irreplaceable.

Get into a habit of writing thank-you notes. Send them to your teachers at the end of the school year, to your coaches at the conclusion of a season, to your friend's mom for writing you a letter of recommendation for that summer lifeguarding job. Don't just send a text. Take the time to write to that special advancer in your life about how much you appreciate who they are, what they have done for you, and the time they have poured into your development. You will never understand the impact your notes have . . . until the day you start receiving thank-you notes yourself.

Previously, we discussed how others influence you. However, it is equally important to remember whom you are influencing. You never know who looks up to you. It could be your little brother or sister. It could be a student in one of the younger classes at your school. It could be a member of your church. Even though you are young, someone is always looking up to you and learning from you. You could be a part of their circle of influence without even realizing it.

I challenge you to live your life with that thought in the back of your mind every day. Choose to live by morals you can be proud of. Decide to make the right choices, no matter who is watching. Show love and care in all that you do. If you choose to live life by these guidelines, I guarantee you will not only live an extremely happy life but also be a positive influence to many for years to come.

We are a product of those who influence us and a creator of those we influence. The circle of influence is a powerful, everlasting cycle; make sure you leave a positive mark.

Summary

- The people you interact with on a daily basis, during different activities, and in all environments make up your circle of influence.
- The people in your circle of influence impact your behaviors, even if you are not aware of it at the time.
- Surrounding yourself with toxic people causes you to think negatively and results in unhappiness.
- Advancers are people who help you climb the ladder of success. Find them. Associate with them. Allow them to help you grow.
- You'll be *amazed* at how far a thank-you note can go.

CHAPTER ELEVEN

What I Would Tell My Teenage Self

~ ♡ ~

"When your mother asks, 'Do you want a piece of advice?'
it is a mere formality. It doesn't matter if you answer yes or no.
You're going to get it anyway."

—Erma Bombeck

Over the years I have frequently asked people, "What would you tell your teenage self?" I find this question interesting because it forces the person to self-reflect on multiple levels. It forces them to think of who they are at this very moment, to remember who they were as a teenager, and to consider the things, people, and lessons that helped them get from their teenage years to the present time. That one question causes them to reflect on a snapshot of many years of their life in one instant.

With that image in their head, oftentimes they smile and then respond almost with a sense of relief by saying something like, "Life would have been a lot easier had I known the lesson I'm about to share." At other times, I see a look of defeat on the person's face, a sign of years of pain and exhaustion they wish they could have avoided. However, while the reaction I receive is different, one thing is the same: They all have something they wish they could have told their teenage selves.

Below you will find some responses I got to this question through my years of research and interviewing. Many would say these pieces of advice are more valuable than any math test, science experiment, or English essay you will ever complete. Below are the lessons that, at their very roots, provide the true meaning of life itself.

It only matters to you now

In our teenage years, we think everything is a life or death situation at this very moment. Everything seems urgent to us. If we are faced with a problem, we truly think the world is coming to an end. If our peers have started rumors about us, we are not only humiliated and terrified, we believe we can never show our faces in public again and that our lives are over.

However, I've interviewed countless women, from their early 20s into their 80s, and unanimously they agreed on one concept: what you think is a big deal now, you won't even remember in a few months or years. The constant stress of teenage drama— the anxieties of rumors being spread, the devastating breakups, and so on—will all fade away just as the clouds fade away after a thunderstorm passes.

I want to be clear that neither these women nor myself are

discrediting the pain and worry you feel during this time in your life. We understand the struggles you are going through, and our hearts break for you. However, we know that you are going to get through it. We know that this pain is only temporary. We know that what you are struggling through right now will only make you a stronger, more confident, and powerful woman down the road. What you are experiencing now is shaping you into the future leader you will be in society one day.

We don't want to act as if you are not hurting. We know you are. However, we want you to realize tough times don't last, tough people do. You are going to be okay. In a few months or years, you will never even remember the drama that you endured and the pain you felt. However, you will be the stronger for it. There is victory on the other side of the battle. Just keep fighting, beautiful.

Your parents are usually right

When I was a teenager, this is the idea I struggled with most. From a young age, I have always had a curious mind and an invincible attitude. In some ways, this is a desirable combination to have. However, for a teenager, if not managed appropriately, it can lead to poor decision-making and a whole lot of trouble. The invincibility I felt led me to think I was always safe, that nothing bad could ever happen to me. No matter how many times my parents would tell me, "Courtney, that is not safe! You are not allowed to do that," or "That is not a good place to be, and you are not going," I would still want to do it. I would argue with them. I would even go to the extent of making pro-and-con lists as to why they were wrong and I was right. Throughout my teen years and young adulthood, I battled my parents constantly on everything from small issues to major life decisions such as which college I would attend.

Looking back, I'm not sure whether I always thought they were wrong just because I was stubborn or whether I objected and defied them because I wanted to be independent: even if I knew the decision I was making was wrong, at least it was my own decision. However, what I do know now, looking back on this, is that *my parents were almost always right!* When I ask adults this question now, they all agree. We push our limits with our parents to see how much rope we can get from them, but later in life we realize they were usually right. Your parents— really, any adults in your life who love you and are helping to raise and care for you—want the best for you, and they have so much more life experience and wisdom under their belts than teenagers do.

I know this is difficult to accept at your age. As I just described, I too as a teenager struggled to accept my parents' advice. However, take it from so many women who have gone before you: Parents are usually right. Don't try to fight it. Just accept it. Embrace it. Grow from it.

Your conscience affects you more than you think

That little voice inside your head that tells you it's probably not a good idea to do something is the most powerful voice there is. That is your *conscience*. The moment you realize how important that voice is will be the moment you start living your life for the better, and honestly, you will end up happier.

Your conscience will remind you of your true values and morals when you're faced with difficult situations. For instance, it is easy to talk bad about someone when everyone around you is doing it. It is easy to stand by and let a friend who has been drinking drive himself home, when the alternative is to be a "downer" and take his keys. The choice to do the wrong thing in those moments—which sometimes includes doing nothing at all—is much easier than the choice to do what's right. However, your conscience will be what saves you, if you listen to it. Listen to that little voice telling you, *This is a bad idea,* or saying, *You are going to feel like crap about yourself if you talk bad about that girl.* Listen to it telling you, *If you don't do something to keep your drunk friend off the road, someone could die!*

When you do wrong, that little voice eats away at your brain, making you feel poorly about yourself. I know you have all experienced this. Maybe you talked about someone and you knew you shouldn't have. That little voice in your head keeps reminding you that you did it and that it was wrong. The sooner you learn that the voice of your conscience is your moral compass, that it will affect you more than you think, and that it will never leave you, the sooner you will start making more positive decisions in your life.

Admitting when you are wrong is a strength, not a weakness

No one likes to admit when they are wrong; it doesn't matter how old you are. However, being wrong is a part of life, just as much as eating, breathing, and sleeping are. If you tell yourself your goal in life is never to be wrong, or never to make mistakes, you are in for a rude awakening and a miserable life. In fact, if you are not making mistakes, you are not growing. Being wrong and making mistakes can be monumental in your development and success, if you allow them to be.

If you are anything like me, you hate being wrong. Even when you know you are wrong, you may continue to argue, just hoping you can make the situation come out in your favor. As a teenager and even early in my 20s, I thought being wrong was a sign of weakness, incompetence, inadequacy, and failure. However, after learning from my mentors, reading many books on personal development, and interviewing hundreds of women, I began to realize admitting you are wrong is a strength, not a weakness. It allows you to self-evaluate, to look at a situation from different perspectives, and to brainstorm ways in which to approach such a situation differently the second time, to come up with a better result.

I fail every day. I get told no every day. I get told, "That is not the right way to do it," every day. But I never see these moments in a negative light. I see them as opportunities every single time: opportunities to grow, opportunities to be better and do things better. I see them as a chance for greater success every time.

I challenge you to start trying to admit when you are wrong. Or, when you do not know how to do something, to admit that you need help. True weakness lies in those who believe they can achieve success on their own. True weakness lies in those who can never see past their own weaknesses and mistakes. However, a person of strength, courage, and influence knows the power of admitting when they are wrong. They see the growth that comes from analyzing a mistake and approaching it from a new angle. They see the wisdom they gain from embracing the mistake and letting it shape them into a stronger version of themselves.

The "different kid" is actually the "cool kid"

Society and social media have defined how the "cool kid" in school looks, dresses, and behaves. For girls, to be "cool" is to have beautiful, long, blonde hair, bright blue eyes, tanned skin, a bubble butt, skinny legs, a narrow waist, and big boobs. The "cool" girl has all the expensive designer clothes and purses. Her makeup is beautifully done every single day, she is always smiling, and she has friends surrounding her at all times. Every guy wants to date her. Every girl wants to be friends with her. For guys, to be "cool" is to be the tall guy with the muscular arms and six-pack abs, the football star who has every girl running up to him after the game on Friday and all the other guys waiting for him to tell them where the party is afterward. These are your typical "cool kids" in school.

If they are the cool kids, then what are the others? What is the girl who has short hair and glasses and loves to read? What is the skinny boy who loves theatre? What is the girl who sits next to you and is always talking about what home science experiment she is doing this week? What is the guy who is constantly researching and working on computers, iPhones, and iPads? To you and your peers, they might be classified as the nerds, the freaks, or the "different kids."

If the women who have gone before you could tell you anything about these kids, they would all agree these "different kids" are actually the "cool kids." These are the kids who are confident in who they are. They do not bow to the pressure of a society that wants to mold them into the idealized image of how a teenager is supposed to look, dress, and act. They are okay with being themselves, happy in their own skin. Most of the time, they are perfectly happy with who you are as well. They don't judge you for how you look or for the passions you have. They realize that everyone is made in their own unique way. They are accepting of not only themselves but others.

Think about some of those "different kids" in your class right now. Close your eyes and picture them. Picture them sitting at their desks in school, reading books you may think are weird. Picture them at lunch, sitting with the other kids you may have labeled "nerds." Now ask yourself: Are they confident? Are they happy? Do they enjoy what they do? Chances are, their confidence is something you wish you had. Their ability to be comfortable with being different is admirable. Their strength to be different in a world that encourages conformity is incredible. These "different kids" are the "cool kids." These different kids are the ones who will not only be highly successful as adults but will be happy and content in their lives.

In fact, some of you reading this right now may be the "different kids." I applaud you. I admire you. Your confidence in who you are and your strength to be yourselves, in a world that judges you and wants you to conform, is incredible. Be proud of your individuality.

Some of you may still be struggling to figure out who you are and where you fit in. In that situation, a lot of teenagers try to fit in with the "cool" kids because it seems safer to conform. But I encourage you to be open-minded toward all people, to see the beauty and value in everyone, to allow the positivity and happiness of others to inspire you. Only when you let yourself appreciate the differences that make us all unique and wonderful can you appreciate and celebrate the unique, wonderful person *you* are!

Thankfulness equals happiness

In our teenage years, we often get caught up in comparing ourselves to our peers or even to celebrities. We look at the things they have that we do not. We sulk about the things they have achieved that we haven't. We constantly desire to have more: more money, more friends, more clothes, more awards, more wins. The list goes on and on. Every day, we either say out loud or at least think about the things we wish we had. Without even realizing it, we begin to feel a sense of sadness about our lives, because the constant reminder of the things we don't have makes us feel as if we are failures in life. Then we begin to tell ourselves we will never have those things, that we are somehow "below" that. This negative mindset begins to consume us, creating unhappiness in our lives. With all the time we spend focusing on the things we wish we had, we typically spend very little time being thankful for the things we do have.

You might be saying to yourself right now, *I do not have anything in life to be thankful for.* Well, let's break that down. If you are reading this sentence right now, either you purchased this book or someone purchased it for you, meaning that someone had money to provide the opportunity for you to read it. Chances are that same individual pays for the home you live in, the electricity that keeps you warm at night, and the water that allows you to shower every day. Take that simple but immense statement and let it sink in for a minute. And think of the other fundamental things you are fortunate enough to have: shelter above your head, food in your belly, and clothes on your back. There are millions of young people who cannot say that.

Over my years of working with young people, focusing on my own personal development, and interviewing people in all walks of life, I have come to realize that the people who claim they are truly happy are those who understand the power of gratitude.

I have a challenge for each of you, to help you practice

thankfulness. Every morning as soon as you wake up, or every evening right before you go to bed, open your journal or the notes app on your phone and write down three things you are thankful for. The key is to physically write them out so you can see them. Don't just think or say them. Those are good too, but there is immense power in seeing right in front of you the things you are grateful for. It can be anything from *I am thankful for the chocolate brownies my mom made last night* to *I'm thankful my parents have the money to take me on vacation every year.* There are no right or wrong answers here. This is not a math exam. It is simply what is in your mind or heart, whatever you are appreciative for. Challenge yourself to do this every day for 30 days.

Chances are, if you stick to this challenge, you are going to see a positive shift in your life. You are going to start feeling calmer during the day. Things that used to typically tick you off, you'll let roll off your shoulders. The heavy weight you felt pressing down on your chest, pressuring you to fit in at school, will lift, and you'll feel as if you can breathe again. You'll catch yourself smiling more. Your mind will seem more at peace. You won't have anxious thoughts pounding into your brain over and over. You will truly feel a sense of happiness taking over your life.

Establish better habits now

You would be amazed at the number of adults I interview, work with, and train who struggle to maintain positive life habits such as nutrition, exercise, and sleep. They wake up every morning, miserably go through their days feeling exhausted, and go to bed every night feeling as if they worked all day yet achieved nothing. Almost all of these people share one common idea with me: they wish they had established better habits at a young age. What you do not realize right now is that your ability to learn new ways of living and to form good habits is the strongest from ages 10 to 18. I am not saying it is impossible for adults to learn and establish new habits in their lives; I'm simply stating it is *easier* to learn and establish them at the age you are right now.

These adults who struggle to go through their daily lives are individuals who at a young age did not practice positive habits such as healthy eating, regular exercise, consistent sleep patterns, or avoiding procrastination. You see the negative effects of this seeping into their adult lives as parents and working citizens in their communities. They hate their jobs. They have poor self-confidence because of their body image. They have no energy to make it through a day, much less to enjoy the little things in life with family and friends.

Does anything about the life I described in the paragraph above sound enjoyable? Of course it doesn't. So don't let yourself get to that point.

I'm going to challenge you to picture yourself in 10 years. Imagine where you are in life. Picture in your mind what job you might have, where you might live. Are you married? Do you have kids?

Now, thinking of that image you have created for your future self, ask yourself the following questions.

· Is my future self happy with the woman I am today?

- Is my future self full of energy, doing a job that I enjoy?
- Is my future self doing positive things for the world around me?

If your answer to these questions was yes, I want you to ask yourself one more question: "What positive habits did my future self possess in order to create their happiness and success?" Trust me: the answer "yes" above did not result from a life of bad habits. In order to live a life of true happiness and success, a person must practice disciplined, positive habits to nourish their life.

Do not let yourself fall into the trap of forming poor habits in your adolescent years that you may find yourself unable to escape later in your life. The earlier you start practicing positive life behaviors, the sooner they become positive habits that will result in a lifetime of happiness, health, and wellness. Make the choice at a young age to set yourself up for success in your life. Do not wait until you are in college or in your 20s. I promise, it is so much harder to start forming them then.

Forgiveness is a gift that keeps on giving

Forgiveness is a difficult thing to do at any age. Think of a time when someone hurt you. Maybe they betrayed you, lied to you, or embarrassed you. Whatever the situation was, ask yourself: Did you forgive this person? If you did, think back to how you felt after forgiving them. Were your mind and heart at peace? Did you feel a sense of relief? If you are still angry with this person, ask yourself how you feel about them. How do you feel in your heart? Is your mind clear, or is it bouncing with frustrated thoughts?

You see, forgiveness is not just a gift of a second chance to the person who has hurt you. Forgiveness is the greatest gift you can give yourself. When you choose to forgive, it creates a sense of peace in your mind and in your heart. When you let anger and resentment build up inside your mind and heart over one situation and one individual, this turmoil leaks over into every aspect of your life. You become irritated, spiteful, and miserable in your thinking and actions. When you do not forgive, you allow the person who has hurt you to control your life. You allow them to control the way you think, feel, and behave.

Instead, if you can find the strength in your mind and heart to forgive those who have caused you pain, you will be giving yourself the greatest gift of all: the gift of a mind and heart free of hatred. You will be giving yourself the ability to freely love and show care toward others. You will be giving yourself the gift of having compassion in your thoughts and behavior. Together, these will provide you with the greatest gift in life: happiness.

Learn to listen

I am an extrovert by nature. Those closest to me would tell you I am outgoing, always smiling, and have never met a stranger. In fact, I've often introduced myself to my seatmate on an airplane and had a conversation with them for two hours straight before landing at our destination. I have never had trouble talking to people. I enjoyed public speaking as a student, I was the first to speak in a team huddle on my sports teams, and my parents would tell you they wished they could have sewn my mouth shut on family road trips.

Growing up, I would have considered myself a good friend, a good leader, and a good listener. However, it was not until my early 20s that I realized I was far from it. When I began my professional career of working in the volleyball industry, I learned quickly that over the years, all I had done was talk. I had never listened.

One of my greatest role models and mentors in life is Ron Kordes. In the volleyball world, he is known nationwide as "The Godfather." He is truly one of the founders of youth volleyball in this country. I have been fortunate enough to play for him since I was six years old, finishing my playing career in his club at age 18 and then working under him as a coach and director. The lessons he has taught me over the years are endless. However, one of his most powerful teachings to me was: *learn to listen.*

Ron explained to me that sometimes people just want to be heard. They do not want an answer. They do not want advice. They simply want to get their thoughts, feelings, and frustrations off their chest and want someone to listen to them. I watched him do this numerous times. I watched him sit in his office and listen to the heartaches felt by athletes, the frustrations felt by parents, and the confusion felt by coaches. Whomever he met with, whatever their age or profession, he began each meeting in the same way: "Tell me what's on your mind." Every time I witnessed this, I was more amazed than the time before. As people would share their stories, their accusations, their frustrations, he would simply listen. Even if a person said things Ron knew were not true, he would not talk. He would allow their voice to be heard. He had mastered one of the greatest skills in life: the ability to listen.

Learning to listen is an extremely difficult task. Also, one must realize there is a difference between listening and waiting your turn to speak. Stephen Covey once said, "Most people do not listen with the intent to understand; they listen with the intent to reply." True listening is not thinking of what your response or rebuttal is going to be, but instead listening intently to every word the other person is saying, taking in their body language, and truly trying to understand where they are coming from. When you can master that, you have truly mastered the ability to be an active listener. Only then will you understand the impact true listening can have on someone's life.

Like I said, listening is not easy, especially for people who tend to be on the extroverted side. I have to remind myself every day, sometimes multiple times a day, to stop talking and just listen. You learn twice as much from listening as you do from talking. Throughout your life, people will forget what you said and what you achieved, but they will always remember the way you made them feel. Make people around you feel heard. Stop talking and listen, and you'll be amazed at the difference it makes in your life and in the lives of those around you.

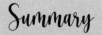

Nine things I would tell my teenage self:

1. It only matters to you now.
2. Your parents are usually right.
3. Your conscience affects you more than you think.
4. Admitting when you are wrong is a strength, not a weakness.
5. The "different kid" is actually the "cool kid."
6. Thankfulness equals happiness.
7. Establish better habits now.
8. Forgiveness is a gift that keeps on giving.
9. Learn to listen.

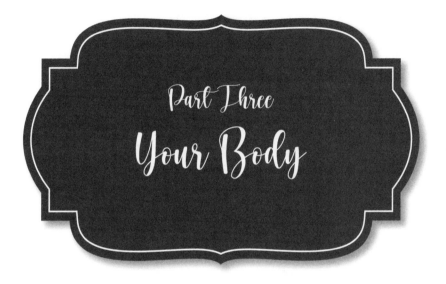

Part Three

Your Body

CHAPTER TWELVE

Habits

"First forget inspiration. Habit is more dependable. Habit will sustain you whether you're inspired or not."

—Octavia Butler

"Watch your thoughts; they become your words. Watch your words; they become your actions. Watch your actions; they become your habits. Watch your habits; they become your character. Watch your character; it becomes your destiny."

—Lǎozǐ (Lao Tzu)

We live in a society today that is constantly looking for the easiest, most convenient and appealing solutions. We also live in a society in which everyone feels that, in order to make positive changes in their lives, they must first be "inspired." Think about it: Every January, when the New Year rolls around, all you hear about for two weeks is New Year's resolutions to get in shape, eat right, or be more present in life. Every year you hear the same resolutions from people who are only motivated to change because it is a new year. Or think about a time someone told you about their current diet, or the new gym/workout program they were doing, or the daily meditation habit they had started. Each of these conversations probably started with the other person telling you about *how* they were inspired to do whatever they are now doing.

Inspiration is important; I'm not discrediting finding motivation via books, blogs, or speakers. What I am saying is that inspiration cannot be the only thing you rely on in life to drive you. At the end of the day, if all you have is inspiration to help motivate you to live a healthy lifestyle, do your homework, or show up to work on time, what happens when your inspiration is gone? What happens if one Wednesday you wake up, it is pouring rain, you didn't sleep well the night before, and all you want to do is stay cuddled up under the covers all day and not come out of your room? What happens then? Do you just stop trying to be the best version of yourself because you are no longer inspired? Do you stop making positive decisions because you didn't listen to a good inspirational podcast this morning or see a motivational post on Instagram?

If you can relate to this, you need to pay attention now more than you have so far in this entire book. Find a spot in your house, a nearby park, or a local coffee shop—anywhere you can escape life's distractions. You need to have 100% focus on the pages that lie ahead. What I'm going to share with you in this chapter will teach you the fundamental principles you need to create success for yourself for the rest of your life. Buckle up, ladies! Let's go on a ride to success!

Often, the word "habit" has a negative connotation. For

example, you might say, "She has a bad habit of biting her nails," or "He has an awful smoking habit." The truth is, though, that if we try, we can also develop *good habits*. A habit, by definition, is a routine or behavior that is repeated regularly and tends to occur subconsciously. You probably already have many positive life habits that you did not even realize were habits, such as brushing your teeth twice a day or taking a daily shower. Activities such as these are something you do repeatedly without thinking. Why do you do them? Your parents forced them upon you as a toddler and you have been doing them ever since. But there are so many more healthy habits than just these two simple daily tasks.

Lucky for each of you, you are in a time of life during which you are like a sponge. Research shows that adolescents have more of the nerve cells that help stimulate actions than adults do. What does this mean, and why should you care? In your adolescent years, it is easier to learn and create habits than for a person your parents' or grandparents' age. You have science on your side. If you can commit to a life of making good choices and establishing healthy habits now, as a teenager, you will be less likely to suffer the kinds of physical, mental, and emotional problems, including addiction and depression, that many adults face today. Use youth to your advantage right now and make a commitment to creating the best version of yourself, because the habits you establish now are the same ones that will accompany you or haunt you into your 20s, 30s, 40s, and so on.

Many of you may be sitting there thinking to yourself, *Okay, this makes sense, but I already think I'm a pretty good person. What else does this crazy lady want from me?* But I'm not talking about your character or your personality, girls. I'm talking about what you do repeatedly that makes you who you are. I'm sure many of you are super sweet girls and always willing to offer a helping hand to others. However, I'll bet you don't eat a balanced, nutritious diet, or get eight hours of sleep every night, or make your bed every day.

Now you are simply thinking to yourself, *I'm done with this book. This is so dumb.* Hang with me, ladies. Let's look at four instrumental habits you are developing in your teenage years that can either make or break your future as an adult.

Nutrition

Right now you might think, *I'm 16. Who cares what I eat? I play a sport, I'm young, and I look fine; I should be able to eat what I want.* Yes and no. Yes, you are young and have a faster metabolism than your adult counterparts, and that allows you to eat a little more and not be affected. However, the eating choices you make in your adolescent years become second nature to you as you progress through the different stages of your life. When you eat, how much you eat, and what you eat all become subconscious because of the habits of nutrition you created in your teenage years.

For example, the teenager who makes a habit of packing their lunch every night before going to bed will be the same college student who packs a lunch instead of choosing from all the fast food options on campus. The teenage student who chooses not to eat a dessert after every single meal will become the mother who does not prepare a dessert every single night of the week for her family. The teenager who packs a banana and peanut butter for an after-school snack before practice will be the adult who packs healthy snacks in their work bag to eat between meetings. Do you see the correlation? What you do now truly does matter. Yes, you may only be 16, but you are creating a habit that is setting you up for either nutritional success or nutritional failure in your future.

Sleep

If I were a betting woman, I'd bet that you probably get five or six hours of sleep per night during the week. You stay up until 2:00 am on the weekends, browsing the internet and texting with your friends. Then you sleep the day away on Saturday and come rolling from your cave of a room against your will around 1:00 pm only because your parents are forcing you to do some chores. Does this sleep pattern sound familiar for any of you?

Research shows the average teenager gets about seven hours of sleep a night. In order for optimal physical, mental, and emotional performance, a teenager's body actually requires about nine hours of sleep. With that said, you can see the majority of teenagers are walking around sleep-deprived on a daily basis. Think about it: Do you have trouble staying awake in class? Do you often feel beyond annoyed by your teachers, parents, and siblings? Do you sometimes feel that your reaction time on the court or stage is slower than normal? Have you ever driven home from school and felt yourself nodding off at the wheel? Chances are you've said yes to one or all of these questions. All of these things have happened to you because you have been sleep-deprived.

Sleep deprivation can cause many cognitive and emotional issues. It can also cause stress on your body that can lead to long-term health concerns. Creating a habit of *good sleep* can impact your life now and forever in a way in which you never imagined possible. If you can get yourself into the habit of falling asleep at relatively the same time each night, waking up to an alarm clock, and not sleeping super-late on the weekends, you will establish for yourself a positive sleep habit that will help you be effective as a college student and as an adult in society.

You may say to yourself, *My body can run off four or five hours of sleep just fine. I just don't require as much sleep as other people do.* Trust me, I get it. I was the same way. All throughout my high school and college career, I was an extremely go, go, go personality type. I was a student athlete who always had a packed schedule. Morning workout, breakfast, class, athletic training for injuries, lunch, study hall, practice, dinner, homework, catch up with friends. There was nowhere in my schedule that allowed for time to sleep. Sleep was my last priority. I did not feel it served any purpose for me, so I made it very small in the grand scheme of my daily schedule.

This four- or five-hour-a-night sleep habit I had created over the years worked for me for a long time. I never saw it as an issue until I was 24. It was 2017, and I was working full time as a club director for KIVA, a volleyball organization in Louisville, Kentucky. My days were packed with scheduling practices, managing coaches, and communicating with parents. On top of my career, I had also met my now-husband that year. We were in the honeymoon phase of dating and would stay up late on the phone, go on date nights throughout the week, and spend entire weekends together. On top of falling head over heels for Will, I was also training for an Ironman. For those of you who may not know what an Ironman is, it is a physical competition where you swim 2.4 miles, bike 112 miles, then run 26.2 miles. You do these all in the same day, one after the other.

As you can imagine, with all of these different things going on in my life, I was a little busy, to say the least. While there were many new things going on in my world, one thing remained constant from my past: my habit of getting very little sleep. I was exercising my brain in my job much more than I had ever been asked to do, my emotional capacity was being tested in my new relationship, and my physical output was far greater than anything I had ever been asked of as a volleyball player. And, for the first time in my entire life, my poor sleep habits caught up with me, in a way I could never have imagined.

One day in April of 2017, after months of grinding away at this new schedule, something happened. I did not wake up for my 5:00 am swim workout. I did not wake up for my 7:00 am breakfast. I did not wake up for my 9:00 am staff meeting, at which I was meant to be leading my coaches. I had slept through over 20 alarms when finally, around 9:30 am, my body woke up. When I realized what time it was, I was in a panic and wanted to get ready quickly and rush out the door, but I did not even have the energy to get up. I was completely exhausted. My throat was scratchy, my body felt weak, and I had the chills. My sister is a nurse practitioner, so I called her and, exhibiting every ounce of energy I had, dragged myself to her office. Right then and there, I was diagnosed with bronchitis. The cure? Ten days on an antibiotic and two weeks of no physical activity.

I thought to myself, *How can this be? No! I don't have time for this. I must train daily for Ironman. I'm overseeing 48 volleyball teams; I must be at practices.* My head was spinning in a thousand directions, but my body was shutting down, telling me no. This was the first experience I ever had with the common saying "running yourself into the ground."

Right now, you are young and energetic and can function on little to no sleep. However, take it from someone who lived that lifestyle for many, many years: I promise you, you can only maintain that way of life for a short period of time. It will catch up with you. Once it does, it is very difficult to change. It took me about two years before I consistently got into the habit of going to bed at 9:00 pm and getting eight hours of sleep regularly. Since I had developed such bad sleep habits as a teenager, I had to work consciously and diligently at detaching from the world and forcing myself to go to sleep earlier for my overall health.

If you can get into the habit now of going to bed at a decent time and actually waking up to your alarm without your parents asking, you are setting yourself up for a successful college career.

How does going to bed early affect what your college future may look like? Think about it. Right now, if you hit the snooze button over and over, Mom or Dad comes in screaming at you to wake up, and then you are out the door 20 minutes later. What happens if you make this a habit? If you rely on your parents to wake you up instead of getting up to the alarm, what will happen when you are in your dorm room alone and the alarm goes off at 7:00 am? What will happen if you hit snooze, oversleep, and miss your 8:00 am class? What will happen is that if you do this repeatedly, you'll end up failing the class. Then your GPA will suffer and prevent you from getting into, say, the nursing school you had been dreaming of. Making sense to you now? The reality is, the sleep habits you create for yourself now directly influence the sleep habits you will have in college and in your adult life.

Exercise

While many adolescents suffer from sleep deprivation, another 18.5% of Americans ages 12–19 suffer from obesity, according to the Centers for Disease Control and Prevention. Unfortunately, today's culture works against us in regard to living an active, healthy lifestyle. Food portions are larger than ever, and technology and convenience remain the center root for all of life's purposes, resulting in a sedentary lifestyle. The simplest of tasks, like having to drive yourself to the grocery, walk around the store, drive home and prepare your meal, have become extinct. Now you can just sit on your couch and order your groceries online, and the store will deliver them right to your doorstep. Due to the convenience-based, least-amount-of-effort mentality society has developed, people's activity levels have dropped drastically, resulting in a skyrocketing level of obesity. The majority of adults think of exercise as a chore, something unenjoyable that they "have" to do in order to stay in shape and healthy.

Fortunately for you, you're at a stage in your life where you can make the literally life-saving habit of exercise a part of your subconscious daily routine now, rather than facing what seems to be an impossible feat to overcome later.

Whether you are an athlete, actress, musician, or avid reader, make the choice now to commit to a healthy lifestyle. Make the choice to be active and live a life of fitness that allows you to experience all the opportunities that lie ahead of you. Choose now not to be just "someone who works out." Instead, make the choice to be a woman who lives a healthy life, a woman who eats a nutritious diet and is physically fit. Make exercising *part of who you are.*

Avoiding procrastination

Procrastination is to a teenager like salt is to pepper or peanut butter to jelly. They simply go together hand in hand. I have yet to meet a teenager who has not said things like, "I'll do that homework tomorrow; it doesn't have to be finished tonight." Or, "I'll clean my room later, Mom." Or, "I'll call Grandma tomorrow." Admit it, you have all said one or all of these things at some point during your adolescent years. Procrastination is so common among teens that oftentimes they don't see it as a negative trait. It's more like a fashion or just a matter of fact: *We are teenagers—that is what we do!*

Unfortunately, if you are one of the teenagers who has developed a general attitude that procrastination is not a big deal, you are in great danger. Procrastination, just like any habit, is so easily formed yet so difficult to break. The issue with procrastination is that it is not a simple bad habit such as biting your nails. Biting your nails is gross, but in the grand scheme of life, it is not going to cause monumental concern. However, procrastination is like treading on a thin sheet of ice that's just waiting to crack beneath you and send you plummeting into icy waters. Procrastination, if allowed to continue, can ruin your life in unimaginable ways.

Right now, your procrastination is simple. For instance, you may put off your math homework assignment until homeroom the next day because it will only take you five minutes to finish. Right now, that works. It is okay. You finish the assignment and all is good. Or you may wait until the weekend to clean your room because you know your mom is out of town for a work trip, so she won't know it's not clean. You get away with it, and all is good. Currently your acts of procrastination do not end in horrific results. In fact, they really don't affect your life that much at all. That is what makes procrastination such a scary habit for teens. Since the effects are minute and go unnoticeable to a teenager, there does not seem to be an issue.

And adolescents often have tunnel vision: they see only what is right in front of them. For example, a teen might think, *If I do not do this homework now, I can browse the internet and catch up with friends.* Seems like a no-brainer. Sold. The issue here does not lie in the direct result of what gets accomplished and what doesn't get accomplished. The issue lies in the habit that is being built by the decision made. Every time a young person chooses to put off something of importance, they are making a choice to replace the task with something that offers *immediate gratification*.

Immediate gratification refers to the instant result gained from something like a decision, a purchase, or an experience. Today's society, no matter what generation, expects immediate gratification. We know what we want, and we want it now. We often do not think about what the consequences, positive or negative, of our actions: we simply act on the fly. However, what we don't realize is that, more often than not, the benefits of *delayed gratification*—of having to wait for or earn something— far outweigh those of immediate gratification. Unfortunately, especially for teenagers with their tunnel vision, but for any generation to some extent, we struggle to see these benefits because we can't see the big picture.

Developing an appreciation for delayed gratification at a young age will help prevent falling into the treacherous outcomes of procrastination. Procrastination can give us the immediate gratification of connecting with friends online, or that delicious chocolate cake, or staying up late hanging with friends, but what we don't realize is that the pleasure of the *now* comes at a very steep price for the *later*.

Picture this: If you knew that putting off homework would

lead to you putting off work assignments at your future job, which would lead to you getting fired, resulting in you being unemployed and not being able to provide food for your family, would you still do it? Or if you knew now that choosing to eat fried food every day for school lunch would lead to obesity and a heart attack at age 28, would you change the way you eat? Or if you knew that staying up late during the week and going out every weekend with your friends, with no consistent exercise during the week, would lead to heart disease or even worse heart failure and death, would you make a habit of exercising and getting more regular sleep?

These examples may seem drastic to you. However, these examples are reality. In the United States, roughly 1.5 million heart attacks occur annually, and over 800,000 deaths occur due to heart disease each year. These horrific numbers are a direct result of habits and life choices that are established in the early years of life. So those "not so big of a deal" choices you are making now truly might be the difference between life and death in the long term.

Understanding the importance of delayed gratification and forming positive lifestyle habits in your teenage years can truly make for a happy and successful adulthood. However, it takes discipline. It takes going against the norms of society. It takes putting off the "want" that you desire now for the life you desire forever. Below, I will provide a few simple steps to create and maintain positive habits now that will pay off for the rest of your life. These steps below can be applied to any habit you choose.

How to build a positive life habit:
- Make it visible
- Make it simple
- Make it measurable
- Make it repeatable

Step 1: Make it visible

In order to create and keep any habit, good or bad, it must be visible. Think about it: people who smoke don't smoke unless they see and have cigarettes. People who overeat do not continue to eat unless they see food. So how do you spin this to "making it visible" in a positive way? Make it unavoidable. Make it noticeable.

For example, if you want to establish the habit of eating a balanced diet every day, set your lunch box on the counter every day when you get home so that it is a constant reminder to pack your lunch before you go to bed. Or if you want to read every night before bed instead of scrolling on Instagram, set your book on your nightstand, where it will stare at you every night when you crawl into bed. Maybe you want to exercise every day after school? Place your workout shoes by your backpack each night as a reminder that you get to work out tomorrow!

Step 2: Make it simple

Making it visible is pretty easy for most people. It is not that difficult to set a lunch box on the counter, or place a book on the nightstand, or set out a pair of shoes. Almost everyone can achieve this first step. It is step two, "make it simple," where many people derail from the track.

In order to form a positive, lifelong habit, it needs to be very simple. Do not overcomplicate things. Oftentimes, in order to "eat healthy," people do crazy or intense diets that are not realistic: the diets are too expensive, too time-consuming, or just plain disgusting. Another mistake people make in regard to developing the habit of fitness is when they go from never exercising a day in their lives to thinking, *I'm going to work out every day at 5:00 am*. I mean, really, whom are you trying to kid here? That will never happen.

Making it simple is the key to success. Do not try to conquer the world all at once. If your goal is to eat a balanced diet, do not go on a fasting diet where you don't eat for 12 hours at a time. And don't try for unrealistic goals like "No carbs or sugar, ever!" Intense diets are not simple enough. When a plan is not simple enough, you will either:

- Never be able to achieve it
- Never be able to stick with it
- Both of the above

I like to live by KISS: "Keep It Simple, Stupid." If you want to eat healthier, start with something small and simple. Instead of eating fried food at lunch every day, pack your lunch from home. Take a sandwich, fruit, almonds, and yogurt. Simply packing your lunch every day will get you into a habit of being prepared with a healthy meal instead of picking the unhealthier fried options at school. It is a simple start that will set you up for long-term success. By choosing to perform such simple tasks, you will turn them into healthy habits that will eventually pile on top of one another, creating an overall positive lifestyle and identity.

Step 3: Make it measurable

As Americans, we live in a world of judgment and comparison. We constantly compare ourselves to others. This can result in negative thinking and outcomes, especially when we compare ourselves to things, experiences, or people that are not realistic. For example, we may compare ourselves to the Victoria's Secret Angels models. This is not realistic, as they have makeup artists, hairstylists, and photo editing to help make their images look flawless. Sorry, but no matter what filter Instagram provides us, we are not going to get our pictures to look like theirs. End of story.

While comparison has some downfalls, many ways of measuring and evaluating ourselves can be beneficial. For example, creating a measurement when trying to establish a positive habit can be extremely helpful in making that habit last. Take exercising, for example. If you say to yourself, *I want to exercise more often*, chances are it will never happen. You have not been specific and given a measurable amount of *how much* you want to exercise. You might exercise here or there, but there is no measure holding you accountable to exercising in order to make it a habit. Instead, if you write down on an index card that your goal is to exercise three days a week and then hang the card on your mirror, where you will see it every morning, you now have a measurable goal.

In order to make that measurable goal successful, you want to make it trackable so that you know whether you have completed the activity. One thing all females seem to have in common is their love for their planners. Think about it: Whether you have a paper planner you carry in your backpack or purse or whether you use an app on your phone, you probably have a planner you look at every day. Make whatever positive habit you are trying to establish trackable in your planner. Put a star in your calendar for each day that you complete your exercise.

This allows you to track the consistency of doing the habit. It allows you every day to see whether you have completed the task. It also helps make the habit something you think about daily, so that it will eventually become subconscious activity. You will just do the habit without thinking, because your habit is now a part of you. It is what you do. It is who you are. Your measurable, trackable goal has been turned into a habit that has ultimately become your identity.

Step 4: Make it repeatable

We can all do anything once. However, being able to repeat something day in and day out is tough. Doing it when we are feeling at our best and continuing to do it even when we are at our lowest of lows is when we have truly established a habit. Step four is the hardest and least achieved step. If it were easy, everyone would do it. This step is what separates the strong from the weak, the disciplined from the lazy, the successful from the failures. This is the step that can separate you from just getting by to having the life you have always wanted.

In order to develop a simple goal into a lifelong habit, it must be something you are able to repeat, meaning you do not make it so extreme there is no humanly possible way to repeat it for an extended period of time. For example, people who live in New York City and do not have an exercise habit set in place are setting themselves up for failure if they tell themselves they are going to run three miles outside every day. Why? Well, do you really think they are going to stick to this habit in the middle of February, when it is four degrees outside with a windchill of negative fourteen? No, didn't think so.

Make your goal something challenging enough to help you improve but easy enough to repeat no matter what the circumstances are. Make it something that is repeatable and flexible, meaning that you can still perform this habit even if you are not in your usual routine or environment.

Let's analyze a goal as simple as reading every night. Make

it noticeable by putting the book on your nightstand. Make it simple: *I will read every night.* Then make it measurable by setting the standard that you must read for 20 minutes every evening. Lastly, make it repeatable. Do not tell yourself you will read three chapters every night. This might be too much, too overwhelming. Make it challenging enough to help you make the improvements you want to see but attainable enough that you will be willing to repeat it day in and day out.

At the end of the day, your life is made up of choices, hundreds of them each day. You are the captain of the ship that is sailing on the journey through your life. There are many routes to take to many different destinations. The choices you make now will establish habits that will either facilitate or burden your sail. The beauty of this world is not just the final island where you arrive. Great magnificence comes with the view along the way. If you follow the steps above, you will establish habits that will allow for a smooth sail. Embrace the decisions. Explore the routes. Most importantly, enjoy the ride.

Summary

Four positive habits every teenager should establish:

- Good nutrition
- Consistent sleep
- Daily exercise
- Avoid procrastination

How to build a positive life habit:

- Make it visible
- Make it simple
- Make it measurable
- Make it repeatable

CHAPTER THIRTEEN

Nutrition

∽♡∽

"Take care of your body. It's the only place you have to live."
—Jim Rohn

According to the Centers for Disease Control and Prevention, 13.7 million American children and adolescents are obese. This means 18.5% of Americans ages 2–19 are living their lives overweight and in danger. In addition to the obesity rate, the US Department of Health and Human Services explains that 3% of American adolescents will suffer from an eating disorder.

In a society that seems to be governed by media and supported by convenience, it is extremely difficult to exercise habits of balance and health. Our social media feeds fill our brains with images of beautiful, sickly skinny female models and tan, chiseled men with more abs than you knew even existed on the human body. We are drowned in these images, but all the while, there is a McDonald's every half mile as we travel to school, work, or a friend's house. From one extreme to the next, American youth face challenges with nutrition on a daily basis.

I was never taught about nutrition in high school or at home. Honestly, it never even crossed my mind. I ate whatever I wanted, whenever I wanted to. It never occurred to me that, as Jim Rohn once said, my body was the only place I had to live. I never considered that the foods I was eating were dramatically affecting the overall well-being of my lifelong home: my body. The decisions you make on a daily basis about what to put into your body directly affect what you get out of your body. As discussed in the previous chapter, habits make up our daily routines. We have habits that we do not even realize we have. If you can learn to make positive nutritional habits, you are guaranteed to see a difference in your mental, physical, and emotional well-being throughout your life.

The first step to understanding nutrition and the balance of it all is to begin with the right mindset. Understand at an early age that you should not let yourself fall into the trap of "dieting." Throughout your life, you will see so many people—parents, aunts and uncles, cousins, friends, and coworkers—get caught up in so many different dieting fads. The end result with all of them is just that: They are fads. They are temporary. Sure, many of them work, and you see almost immediate results. However, the common denominator with all of them is they are temporary, whether they're 21 days of no sugar or 30 days of eating whole foods. None of these "diets" put into place the two factors needed for healthy eating: longevity and consistency.

We live in a society where people want immediate results

127

while putting in the least amount of work possible. They see no value in delayed gratification. This could not be more apparent than in the approach so many Americans take to their nutritional lives. They want immediate results, usually weight shed instantly. However, they do not want to change the way they eat or exercise. While Americans jump from different diet fad to different diet fad, they are all missing the ultimate answer. Weight loss is not found in crash diets, and more energy is not found in going keto. The physical results desired by most are found in the understanding that nutrition is a lifestyle, not a fad.

The sooner you can wrap your head around the idea of fueling your body every day with balanced, nutritional foods, the sooner you will be setting your life up for excellence. I share this chapter with you in the hope that the education you receive from the understanding of nutrition as a lifestyle will assist you in making better choices for yourself, resulting in a lifetime of health and happiness.

When deciding to make the commitment to a lifestyle of healthy nutrition, there are three important things to remember:

- Balanced eating is important
- Failing to prepare is preparing to fail
- Nutrition is a lifestyle

Balanced eating is important

Unlike with many crash diets, when you live a life of healthy nutrition, you still get to eat everything you like! What I mean by this is that many diets will take out carbohydrates completely or will say that for a month you can only eat foods that contain fat, or no sugar. When you commit to a life of balanced eating, you still get to take in foods from all the food groups, just in moderation. Life is all about moderation. Is eating a brownie once a week really going to make you gain 10 pounds? No. But eating a brownie after every meal for a year is probably not going to help you lose weight, and your cholesterol is likely to suffer. Start at an early age not only understanding the importance of balanced eating but also appreciating it and allowing it to become what you do daily, not just a temporary phase.

Many of you may not understand what "balanced eating" even looks like. Let's take a look at the different food groups and their nutritional impact on our lives. Probably you have learned about the Food Pyramid at some point during your academic careers. You have also probably heard the words carbohydrates, protein, vitamins, minerals, and fats in reference to foods. However, I would bet that many of you do not know where the foods you eat daily fall into the pyramid or what they are made up of. Take a look at the simple chart below to get a better understanding of what you eat and what effect it has on your body.

129

TYPE OF FOOD	EXAMPLE OF FOOD	MAIN NUTRIENT
Grains	Bread, Pasta	Carbohydrates
Meat	Chicken, Steak	Protein
Fruits	Blueberries, Apples	Vitamins
Vegetables	Carrots, Salad	Vitamins
Dairy	Milk, Cheese	Calcium and Vitamin D
Desserts	Brownies, Cake	Sugar

Now, understand that this chart is a mere snapshot on the most basic level of different foods and their effects on the human body. It is not my goal to make each of you nutritional wizards. My goal is for you simply to have an understanding of the foods you eat and how they will impact your life today, tomorrow, and five years down the road. It is important to understand that all the food groups are important, and cutting any of them out forever is not the answer to a lifetime of nutritional excellence. Having each group in moderation is the key to seeing everlasting results of sustained weight, energy, and happiness. If you can commit to eating a balanced diet every day, starting now, you will start a habit of nutritional stability for which you will be forever grateful.

failing to prepare is preparing to fail

As we have discussed previously in this book, we live in a world shaped by convenience. We like things done for us, in a quick manner where we receive instant gratification. For example, it is

WHAT IT PROVIDES

Provides sustained energy
Builds muscle
Strengthens immune system
Reduces the chances of getting diseases
Builds and maintains strong bones
Gives you a big smile

much easier to go through the drive-thru at McDonald's to get lunch on a Saturday before meeting your friends at the mall than it is to make a salad with grilled chicken at home. I get it. However, there is a way to create this sense of convenience for yourself, and it will work in your favor in regard to nutrition.

Oftentimes, we choose convenient food options simply because we do not have anything else to choose from. For instance, let's say that after a long day at school you head straight to theatre rehearsal. You have no snacks packed. What do you do? Purchase a Coke and a candy bar from the concession stand at the studio. This is why I say that failing to prepare is preparing to fail. If you prepare healthy meals and snacks ahead of time, then it is convenient for you to eat them instead of being forced to purchase the unhealthy options all around us.

Planning your meals and snacks ahead of time can feel like a huge burden. It may seem as if it will take too much of a time commitment the night before. At first, yes, it will. However, as with any habit, if you can be disciplined for 21 days, you will make it easier to turn it into a habit, ultimately turning the habit into your lifestyle: who you are, what you do.

Begin small, with this: Pack yourself a healthy afternoon snack for the next day every night before bed. Choose a snack that will give you energy and nutrients before your extracurricular activities. Some examples of healthy snack options are almonds, celery and peanut butter, strawberries, or yogurt with blueberries. Be disciplined in packing this snack every single night; that way, you have the convenience of eating this in the afternoons.

From there, take it a step further: begin packing your lunch every night. Some of you younger ones may need assistance with this from your parents, as they are the ones purchasing and cooking your meals. Whether you pack it alone or with the assistance of an adult, learn to pack a balanced lunch for yourself every day. Lunch options could include a turkey sandwich, grilled chicken, salad, carrots, a banana, yogurt, string cheese, blueberries, or strawberries.

By preparing a healthy lunch option the night before, you are setting yourself up for success the next day. It is when we do not plan ahead that we often find ourselves in situations of purchasing the pizza and chocolate chip cookie at school because it is easy, convenient, and right in front of our face. It is much easier to be disciplined and eat a healthy, balanced option when we have that option right in front of us.

I would love to tell you I have always lived a disciplined life in regard to nutrition. However, I'd be lying. My understanding of food and its impact on me did not come until my college years.

Growing up, I never packed a healthy snack, I ate every single meal from school, and I had a bowl of ice cream every night before bed. It was not until I met my strength and conditioning coach in college that I began to understand the value of nutrition and the delayed gratification it would provide me. He helped me understand the importance of preparation and how a lack of preparation would lead me to failure. He was the one who inspired me to pack my lunch every day in college. Now, many years later, I pack my lunch every single day for work, I do not leave the house to run errands for the day without a healthy snack, and I never go on a road trip without healthy options packed.

I have watched many friends and family members go through toxic struggles with their weight. I've seen crash diets resulting in a skinny image but a forced smile, because deep within themselves, the person knew they were not truly happy or healthy. I have seen friends completely let themselves go and suffer from obesity because they couldn't be disciplined with their eating. I am fortunate that I have never had to experience these struggles of body image and eating because of my early understanding of the value of nutrition and the impact it would play on me in the long term. I have never had to battle weight issues, because I made the commitment early on to make a habit of preparation. I did not allow myself to fall into the vicious cycle of lack of preparation that leads to poor food choices. I made an early commitment to nutritional discipline, and that has created physical and nutritional stability for me as an adult.

If I was able to change from the teenager eating Oreos and milk in the bathtub to a woman packing a lunch every day for work, you can too. However, do not wait until you're an adult to eat healthy. Make the decision now to prepare for success. Choose now to understand the importance of nutrition and the effect it has on your physical, mental, and emotional well-being.

Nutrition is a lifestyle

In conclusion, nutrition is a lifestyle, not a fad. The earlier in life you can understand this, the less frustration and disappointment you will encounter. So many people try diet after diet and oftentimes see results but can't keep the weight off. They never truly feel that they have sustained energy. Why? Their diet was temporary. They ate healthy for a period of time, then stopped. It is not rocket science. People spend hours upon hours researching different diets and trying different foods, only to be let down in the long run. The answer to weight management, energy, and happiness is very simple: Nutrition is a lifestyle. It is not momentary.

If you truly want to see long-term results of maintaining a healthy weight, feeling energetic, and being emotionally stable, you must make the commitment to healthy nutrition being a part of your lifestyle. Once you can accept that eating healthy is not something that you do, it is who you are, you will be on the path to a lifetime of health and happiness.

Summary

- Nutrition is a lifestyle, not a phase.
- Nutrition is not about getting immediate results, like losing 10 pounds in a week or getting six-pack abs by taking a pill. It is about having lifelong health and happiness.
- Nutrition is not a diet, it is balanced eating every day.
- Not preparing your food ahead of time will lead to poor food choices.

Part four

Your Mind

CHAPTER FOURTEEN

Leadership

༄

"Leaders are made, they are not born. They are made by hard effort, which is the price which all of us must pay to achieve any goal that is worthwhile."

—*Vince Lombardi*

All your life, you will hear the word "leadership." Think about it: you have probably already heard it from many people in different environments and in various ways. Leadership is something your parents, teachers, coaches, instructors, and role models are constantly encouraging you toward. I'm sure you have heard phrases such as "You are a natural-born leader, so go out and make a difference in the world," "In order to make it in the world you have to become a leader," and "Don't settle for being a follower; be brave and become a leader."

I assume many of you, deep down, want to be leaders. You just aren't sure how to begin. You may be asking yourself, *How do I become a leader? What does a leader look like? Where do I start?* It seems a lot easier to let someone else do all the work. You are right. There is nothing easy about being a leader. If it were easier to be a leader than a follower, everyone would be doing it. People do not like to do hard things. People do not like to be different. However, you are unique. You have the capability of being a great leader and influencing in a positive way, but you have to believe it. You have to find that leadership buried deep within you and bring it to the surface. When you have a passion, you make it your life's purpose. It takes true leadership and courage to live it out in a powerful way that serves others.

Often, when people think of a leader, they think of the super-loud, outgoing, organized, smart, and friendly individual who gets along with everyone. However, a leader is not a cookie-cutter image. Leaders have all types of personalities. Some are outgoing; some are quiet. Some are highly organized; others are a bit all over the place. Some have a ton of energy; others are more quiet and reserved. Do not slot yourself as a leader or not a leader based on your personality. I truly believe leaders are not born; instead, they are made. People can lead with any type of personality if they have mastered the skill sets required to execute effective leadership.

Confident, not cocky

Many people never achieve leadership because they let their egos get in the way. Some of the best leaders in the world have come tumbling down from the top in failure due to their own cockiness. One of my favorite quotes on separating confidence from cockiness is by Mila Kunis: "Knowing who you are is confidence. Cockiness is knowing who you are and pushing it down everyone's throat." True leaders are confident about who they are. They are firm in their morals, values, and beliefs. They are clear on their visions. They are aware of their strengths and weaknesses. They capitalize on those strengths, and they accept their weaknesses and work to improve them by surrounding themselves with people who are better at those areas than they are. They are always eager to learn, improve, and grow. They never believe they have arrived at the top. They understand that success is never achieved alone. Leaders understand there is always someone helping them achieve whatever goals they have set. They realize there is always another member to add to their army, making it a stronger unit. They realize there is strength in numbers and that two heads are better than one. They know themselves inside and out.

Although a leader knows exactly who they are, they do not constantly brag about who they are and what they have achieved. True leaders let their work, achievements, and impact on society speak for themselves. If you want to be a good leader, what do you do? Shut your mouth, put your head down, and get to work. Strive to be great through your actions. Make a difference in people's lives and in the world as a whole. Develop authentic, loving relationships. Impact others in a positive way. If you can do that, your confidence will shine. You won't have to tell anyone, trust me. Confidence, not cockiness, is what grabs the respect of everyone around you. Remember, confidence is beautiful. Go out and show the world your true beauty.

Actions speak louder than words

A successful leader never asks those they are leading to do anything they would not do themselves. For example, if you are trying to lead a school project successfully, you won't ask someone to do any portion of the work that you would not be willing to do yourself. Another example could be in a sports setting. Let's say there are kids on your team who are younger, and you feel that you have seniority over them because you are older. A poor leader would use their age and power to make others do some of the dirty work, such as making the younger kids set up the court for practice or carry everyone's water to the locker room after the game. If you truly want to be a leader, lead by example, not by your voice. You will immediately gain respect from those you are leading when they see you put in the same work yourself.

Develop relationships

No matter what you are doing or whom you are leading, you must develop positive relationships with people if you expect to lead them. People buy into a person long before they buy into an idea. Through my years as a coach, I have learned that a kid will do anything in this world for me, run through a wall for me, spend hours practicing the same skill over and over and over again, as long as they believe that I love them, I care about them, and I believe in them. The strong relationships I have built with my athletes allow me to lead them. They trust me and they believe in me, so ultimately they will follow me.

Leadership is bringing out the best in another person to help them achieve a shared vision. Great leaders make those around them better in all that they do. If you truly want to be a great leader, start asking yourself, *What kinds of relationships do I have with those I am trying to lead? Do they like me? Do I treat them well? Do they think I work hard?* Truly evaluate how you treat those around you. Throughout your life, people will forget what you said or what you did, but they will never forget how you made them feel. Begin now in creating positive relationships with those around you. Treat people with respect. Make them feel loved. Show them you care about them. Allow them to know that you are interested in who they are and what they do. Until you develop true, authentic relationships with people, you will never lead. You will simply be walking alone.

Listen, learn, lead

People who feel heard are invested. Part of developing relationships with those you are leading is to truly listen to them. Listen to their passions, their ideas, and their visions. A couple of things happen when you listen to the people you lead. For one thing, you learn a lot about them as individuals. You begin to learn what they enjoy, what motivates them, how they learn. This will help you down the road, when you are trying to lead them to achieve a goal. By listening to them, you also instantly gain respect from them, and they feel connected to you. Everyone loves to talk about themselves. If you give a person a chance to be heard by you, and if you truly listen and engage in conversation

LIVING IN REAL TIME

with them, you will immediately gain a follower.

Picture this in a real-life situation. Let's use a group project in school as an example. There are four people in your group, and you are trying to take on the role of leader. Your end goal for the project is to get an A. Before you just start assigning who should do which tasks, take the initiative to go around the circle and ask each person what they would enjoy doing in regard to the project. For example, do they like to write, draw, take pictures, or speak? Try to listen and learn what your group members' passions are. From there, you can realize what their strengths are. You will start to see what they do not feel comfortable with. People will perform at a higher level when they are doing something they enjoy. So make life easier on everyone: Do not try to force someone to do something they hate or don't feel comfortable with. Find what they are good at and let them run with it.

Understand strengths and weaknesses

If you want to lead those around you to achieve a shared vision, you must understand people's strengths and weaknesses. Think back to the picture we painted in the previous section, regarding the group project. After you listen to your group mates and learn what they enjoy, it is easy to see what their strengths and weaknesses are. If there is a person in the group who says they are mortified by public speaking, news flash: They probably aren't going to be too great during the presentation. So don't assign them a huge speaking part. Instead, maybe they enjoy taking pictures. Use their strength of photography and creativity and let that person take the pictures that will be displayed in the final presentation.

The sooner in your life you realize everyone has something they can bring to the table, the sooner you will become a successful leader. Great leaders set their followers up for success by letting them be great at what they are great at. Leaders are able to listen and learn what people's strengths and weaknesses are and put them in positions where they can thrive by carrying out their strengths. People enjoy doing what they are good at, and they enjoy it when they see success. If you want those you lead to continue to work with you toward a common goal, continue to set them up for success. Find ways for them to execute their strengths in service of your common goal. The people you lead will likely continue to follow you if you're constantly giving them opportunities to do what they enjoy, to achieve tasks they can feel proud of, and to see their accomplishments.

The best leaders in the world realize that it takes a team to achieve anything great. They know success is never achieved alone. Leaders understand that every member of a team can contribute in a positive way. Leadership is the ability to figure out another person's worth and help bring out the greatest version of them. Always remember that everyone has a strength deep within. You, as a leader, have to help bring that strength to the surface. Once you do, just sit back and watch the person shine. It's a beautiful thing.

fear of failure is fatal

"Failure is not the opposite of success; it's part of success."
—*Arianna Huffington*

I fail every single day. As a coach, there are days I do not give my athletes everything they need. As a writer, sometimes I sit and stare at a blank page and fail to write anything of meaning. As a wife, sometimes I let my own worries consume me and fail to show love to my husband. Every day I make mistakes. Every day I fall. Every day I fail. However, with every mistake, I learn a new way that does not work, getting me one step closer to the way that does. With every fall, I have the opportunity to stand back up with strength. Every time I fail, I get one step closer to success.

It took me a very long time to understand that the fear of failure was fatal to my development and success. Growing up, I thought failure was a sign of weakness. I thought only weak people made mistakes. I thought successful athletes, celebrities, and leaders in the world were perfect. They never failed. Somehow they had figured out the recipe for perfection.

During my journey of writing this book for you, I had a mission to help you understand leadership and how to achieve it. I interviewed successful leaders from all walks of life, all ages, genders, and ethnicities. While the people I interviewed had their differences, they all shared one common experience: They had failed many times. I was shocked to hear all of them share with me so openly about their failures. However, what I was even more floored by was how thankful they were for their failures. Every leader I worked with explained how their failures had led to their successes.

I hope you can understand that in order to achieve something great, you must take risks. With risk comes the unknown. With the unknown comes trial and error. With trial and error come mistakes. With mistakes come failure. With failure comes wisdom. With wisdom comes success. Failure is part of the journey to achievement. Each failure is a little victory in realizing a way that does not work, leading you to a different option that might just be the one that does. If you fear failure, you are setting yourself up for defeat before you even start. Once you can fight away the fear, you can fly.

Accept responsibility

Great leaders take responsibility not only for their own actions but for the actions of their teams. They see no separation between themselves and the people they lead. They see all of them on an equal playing field, competing for a common goal. If one part of the process fails, they all fail. A leader takes responsibility for every part. Together they succeed or together they fail.

Learn to accept responsibility for all aspects of your goal. When you take responsibility, people notice. Your followers sense your connection to them. They feel your genuineness. By taking responsibility as a leader, you will motivate people to work harder, smarter, and more effectively. Accepting responsibility brings you one step closer to achieving success.

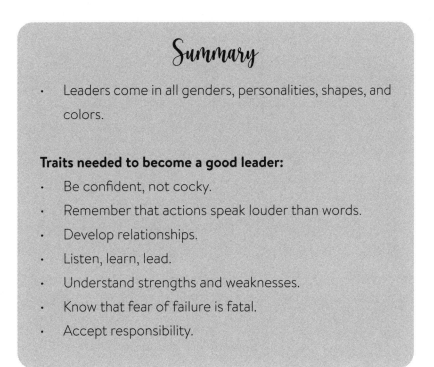

Summary

- Leaders come in all genders, personalities, shapes, and colors.

Traits needed to become a good leader:
- Be confident, not cocky.
- Remember that actions speak louder than words.
- Develop relationships.
- Listen, learn, lead.
- Understand strengths and weaknesses.
- Know that fear of failure is fatal.
- Accept responsibility.

CHAPTER FIFTEEN

Conflict

"A lot of problems in the world would disappear if we talked to each other instead of about each other."
—Author unknown

Chances are, you are beginning to learn life is full of conflicts. I would say it is safe to say you have experienced conflict on a daily level yourself, such as the conflict you feel when you think your teacher is always picking on you, or when a boyfriend breaks up with you, or when two of your friends are fighting and asking you to pick sides. Conflict truly is everywhere. Conflict surrounds us at an early age, and unfortunately, you will be faced with conflict for the rest of your life.

However, it doesn't have to be as terrible as it sounds. Conflict will only consume you in a negative way *if* you allow it to. In fact, facing conflict head-on will not only help solve the issue at hand but will actually help you grow into a stronger young woman. Albert Einstein once said, "In the middle of difficulty lies opportunity." Facing conflict head-on is extremely difficult. However, with it comes the opportunity for solutions, growth, and peace. The earlier in life you learn how to face conflict and resolve it in a positive way, the more strongly you are setting yourself up for long-term success and happiness. Below you will find steps to apply to any conflict situation you face.

Accept that there is a conflict

The first step in resolving conflict within your life is accepting that the conflict is there. Conflict is a reality of life. It is always going to arise. It is not going to go away because you close your eyes, hide, or run away from it. The sooner in life you accept this fact, the sooner you will be able to solve issues in a successful way for all involved.

Think of the conflict you probably have churning inside of you right now. Is it your best friend spreading a rumor about you at school? Is it a broken relationship with your mother? Is it that you hit your little brother last night because he stole your phone and was reading your texts? Whatever it might be, think about it: It's not going anywhere. You can choose to ignore the fact that your friend has spread rumors about you, but in the back of your mind, you are still going to be angry at her and feel hurt in your heart if you don't talk to her about it. You can continue to live every day of your life with hatred toward your mother, but the reality is, she is the only mother you will ever have. Are you going to choose to let that relationship be buried because of your inability to face the conflict? You can go through the next week thinking that if you ignore the fact that you hit your brother, he will disappear, but news flash: He lives in the same house as you. He's not going anywhere.

So the reality is, conflict is everywhere. Don't ignore it. Don't hide from it. Don't run from it. Face it. Accept it.

Deal with the problem, not the person

Oftentimes, when conflict arises, the emotions that come to the surface are immediately targeted toward the person, not the problem. For example, if your best friend starts a rumor about you, immediately you are angry with your friend instead of at the fact that there was a rumor started. In order for successful conflict resolution to take place, you must maintain focus on the problem, not the person. Don't allow things to get personal. Start working toward a solution to eliminate the problem and move forward in a positive way.

Consider how you feel

Before you are able to make any steps toward solving conflict, you must first be very aware of how *you* feel. This is a step that many people never take the time to truly evaluate. Why? It is much easier to be reactive and fire off angry words toward someone instead of sitting down, closing your mouth, and thinking about how this situation has truly made you feel.

A couple of things happen when you think about how a conflict is making you feel. First, it prevents you from being reactive and potentially saying something you don't mean. One of the greatest lessons I've learned in life is the 24-hour rule: When someone has done or said something that sparked immense negative emotions in you, do not allow yourself to respond to that person in any way—face to face or by phone call, text, social media post, email, or anything else—until 24 hours have passed. During this 24-hour phase, a few things miraculously happen:

- You give yourself time to let the emotions settle down.
- You are able to think about the problem, not the person.
- You are able to think about how *you* feel.
- You are able to address the problem in a *logical*, versus an *emotional*, state.

Second, asking yourself how you feel allows you to truly understand what emotions you have and where you stand in regard to the conflict. Ask yourself, *What feelings do I have right now? Am I angry, hurt, embarrassed, sad, frustrated, or annoyed?* Once you know what your feelings are, you are ready for the next step in the conflict resolution process.

Communicate how you feel

In order to move toward a solution, you must communicate to the person how you are feeling. You should already know what you are going to share with this person, because in the previous step, you reflected on how you felt. However, you might not know *how you are going to communicate this.* Communication during times of conflict is extremely difficult, especially during your teenage years. I know what is going through your head right now: *I can't text her and tell her how I feel. She will send the text to all of our friends, and I will look like a complete nerd.* Technology and social media have made dealing with conflict a beast to tackle. Quite honestly, my heart breaks for you guys, because you are living in an era that almost seems impossible to survive through. However, I promise you can do it. You can communicate how you feel, and you can solve conflicts.

I could lie to you and tell you it would be easy, but you already know that would be a lie. So I'm not going to sugarcoat it. Here it is, black and white facts: Communicating how you feel during a conflict can feel extremely uncomfortable. However, I truly believe God gives his hardest battles to his toughest soldiers. You are His little warrior, ready and able to take on the battle. You can do it. Just follow these steps:

- Communicate how you feel through words, and always face to face when possible. Never through texting. In your generation, this is extremely tough to do. You were born into a generation that I like to call "screen babies." Many of you could operate a cell phone before you were three years old. You have spent your entire lives with screens in hand. This explains why you are programmed to communicate through texts, Snapchat, or TikTok. Communicating through a screen comes more naturally to you than having a face-to-face conversation. I understand. However, if you do not communicate how you feel to someone face to face, you will never learn how to deal with an uncomfortable situation, communicate using both words and body language, and work through a problem toward a positive solution. Trust me when I tell you, learning at a young age to communicate your feelings in person, instead of taking the easy way out by staying shielded behind a screen, will pay off for you immensely in the long run!

- Use "I" statements whenever possible. When you are communicating your feelings, try to use "I" as much as possible instead of pointing the finger and saying "you." For example, here are some "I" statements:
  - I feel sad when I hear rumors that you have spread about me.
  - I felt betrayed when I realized you had lied to me.

  These are examples of not using "I" statements:
  - You made me cry because you spread lies about me.
  - You are such a liar!

- Explain what feelings and thoughts you have about the situation at hand. Use clear adjectives and descriptions about your feelings. Try to maintain a calm tone. And stick to the present; do not drag old fights into the current conversation.

Practice active listening

Once you have communicated how you feel, it is time to listen to the other person. Listening is a skill that many never master.

However, some of the smartest, wealthiest, and most successful leaders in the world claim that their success comes from a diligent focus on listening. When we listen, we gain wisdom. When we listen, we make people feel connected to us. At the end of the day, connection and acceptance are truly what everyone is looking for. One of my favorite quotes is from the philosopher Diogenes: "We have two ears and only one tongue in order that we may listen more and talk less."

When trying to solve a conflict, you must actively listen to the other person. This means you must provide them with 100% of your attention while they are speaking. Listen to them to truly hear what they are saying. Do not be thinking of your next response for the entire time their mouth is moving. Listen to their words. Look at their body language. Try to put yourself inside their heart and soul and feel what they feel. Only when they have finished speaking should you even begin to think of your next response.

find options together

After both of you have had the chance to speak and express your feelings, it is time to start working toward a common solution. During this time, you will want to come up with different options to fix the problem. Sometimes, the solution might be as simple as one of you apologizing and both of you agreeing to forgive each other. Other times, it may require the person who spread a rumor to go to the people they spread it to and admit that it wasn't true, in order to gain respect and trust back from the person they hurt.

The options available will vary based on the conflict. It is important to discuss as many options as possible together. Working together and learning to negotiate what is best for both people involved will help create a win-win situation for everyone. At the end of the day, all you are looking for is to resolve the conflict!

Learn to say and accept "I'm sorry"

Admitting you are wrong, and apologizing, are not signs of weakness. In fact, the first person to apologize is the bravest. "I'm sorry" is the best last thing you can say in any dispute. The words "I'm sorry" are almost always guaranteed to end a conflict and allow both people to move forward. Learn to apologize when you are at fault, and learn to forgive the person who says they are sorry. Learn to move forward in peace and happiness. One of my favorite quotes sums up apologies beautifully: "The first to apologize is the bravest. The first to forgive is the strongest. The first to forget is the happiest." Be brave and apologize. Be strong and forgive those who have made mistakes. Be happy and move on with your life.

Summary

- Conflict will be a part of your life for the rest of your life.
- The sooner you learn how to manage conflict, the greater happiness and success you will experience.

Conflict resolution steps:
- Accept that there is a conflict.
- Deal with the problem, not the person.
- Consider how you feel.
- Communicate how you feel.
- Practice active listening.
- Find options together.
- Learn to say and accept "I'm sorry."

CHAPTER 16

No Guarantees

On February 14, 2020, my life changed forever. I was driving to Kansas City, Missouri to coach in a volleyball tournament. Traveling for volleyball tournaments is something I have done for 20 years, first traveling as an athlete and now as a coach. This drive seemed no different than the thousands of miles I had traveled before. It was an unusually beautiful February day, with the sun beaming down. Two other coaches accompanied me on the drive.

I received a call around 3:00 pm from Justin Prather, father of one of the athletes on my team. It was a call I will never forget; the fear in his voice will forever be planted in my mind.

"Have you talked to Lesley or Rhyan?" he asked. Lesley was his wife; Rhyan was his 12-year-old daughter.

".I have not," I replied.

Justin explained to me that Lesley and Rhyan had left Louisville around 7:00 am in Lesley's minivan, accompanied by another athlete on my team, Kacey McCaw, and her mother, Carrie McCaw. The four should have arrived in Kansas City by that time, but Justin had not heard from either his wife or his daughter since 10:30 am. And he could see from tracking their phones that they were still in St. Louis.

I immediately hung up the phone and called Kacey's father to see if he had heard from Carrie or Kacey. At first, he did not answer. My heart began to race as I reached out to members of our team to ask if they had heard from the girls. No one had spoken to them since 10:30 am. I frantically called the hotel to ask whether they had checked in. They had not.

As my body began to tremble with fear, Kacey's father Dave returned my call. All I can remember is hearing him sob. The only words I could make out were "They are all gone."

Carrie McCaw, age 44, Kacey McCaw, age 12, Lesley Prather, age 40, and Rhyan Prather, age 12, had all been killed in a car crash on I-64 right outside St. Louis, when a pickup truck broke through the cable barrier and overturned before striking the minivan head-on, taking the lives of all four beautiful souls.

That evening was a complete blur as I tried to come to terms with the reality that two of my athletes and their mothers were gone forever. It seemed like a nightmare. Surely I would wake up and Kacey and Rhyan would run out onto the court tomorrow morning for our 8:00 am match, with their beautiful smiles and light-hearted spirits, while Carrie and Lesley would be in the stands cheering them on, beaming with pride in their daughters.

But this was no nightmare. This was the reality that there are no guarantees. We are not guaranteed the next day, the next hour, or the next minute. The only guarantee we have is that at some point, all of us will pass away. Because of this, we each should choose to live life in the present moment. Do not wait until tomorrow,

158

next week, or next year to start living a life of happiness, helping others, and spreading love. The reality is that you might not have tomorrow, next week, or next year.

It was not until the tragic accident of my four angels that I realized the truth and depth of living in the "now" and showing others love in all that you do. In the days, weeks, and months following the accident, I was overwhelmed by a roller coaster of emotions. I remember walking into the hotel in Kansas City hours after I had heard the news. We brought our club together in a ballroom for a prayer service. As I looked around, hundreds of athletes and their families were clinging to one another in shock and helplessness as they tried to come to terms with the fact that they had lost four members of their very close-knit volleyball family. After the prayer service, we coaches brought the eight remaining athletes on our team together to discuss what they wanted to do in regard to the weekend. Did they want to play or go home?

To us, as adults, this decision seemed like a no-brainer. Of *course* we would go home and not play. These kids had just lost two of their teammates and those teammates' mothers. They were beyond devastated and in shock. Just like any other sane adults would, we believed there was no way the kids would have the mental or emotional capacity to compete.

However, with courage in their veins and honor in their hearts, the remaining 12-year-old athletes said they wanted to play in the tournament in loving memory of their two deceased teammates and their teammates' mothers. These players had courage and resilience that inspired athletes, parents, coaches, and spectators nationwide.

For the next three days, these eight athletes competed in one of the most competitive club volleyball tournaments in the country. At every match, they were given flowers by other teams. Their opponents had written Kacey's and Rhyan's names on their wrists and wore ribbons in their memory, with the girls' numbers on them. The outpouring of love and support to our team was overwhelmingly generous and appreciated. And that love and support did not stop when we left Kansas City. For weeks and months to follow, volleyball clubs nationwide, news stations, and college programs all over the country sent cards, flowers, and donations in honor of our four angels we had lost.

As the accident of the McCaws and Prathers hit the national news, I felt as if I were a bystander in a subway as people and places hustled by me all day and night. Everything was a blur. As my emotions and thoughts were bouncing back and forth by the minute during those first few weeks, one thing remained consistent: their love. No matter where my mind took me, it would always come back to realizing the love Carrie, Kacey, Lesley, and Rhyan had for everyone and everything they did in life. As I looked at the broken hearts of hundreds of thousands of people, I could see the true reflection these women had on so many lives.

They were women of true beauty, inside and out. Their smiles were contagious. Their love for others was shown in their daily actions. Their energy was noticed by all as they lived their lives to the fullest every day. Their passion for the game of volleyball was undeniable. Their leadership inspired so many people of all ages. In such a short time on this Earth, these women influenced and inspired so many because they truly lived their lives knowing there were no guarantees. They did not wait until tomorrow, or next week, or next year to love others. They did not wait for the next family Christmas to visit their grandparents. They did not wait until problems got so bad they could not take it to build their relationships with God. No, they lived every day of their lives with positive attitudes, contagious smiles, love for all people with whom they crossed paths, helpful hands to those in need, and unquestionable faith in Jesus Christ. They were true walking angels on this Earth, loving, leading, and inspiring.

They were an example to each of us that there are no guarantees. Any day could be our last. We must spend every moment we have with peaceful minds, loving hearts, and undeniable faith.

CHAPTER 17

Plans Change

~ ♡ ~

"Life is what happens to us while we are making other plans."

—Allen Saunders

As teenagers, we often have a vision of what we think our life will look like as adults. *I'm going to graduate from high school, go to medical school at the University of Alabama, meet a Southern gentleman, open up a dermatology practice, get married, have three kids, and live happily ever after.* Some of you have a vision that you will start your own business, be a professional athlete, or be a performer in a Broadway show.

I get it. I've been there. As a 16-year-old Catholic schoolgirl in Louisville, Kentucky, I believed I would graduate from Assumption High School, play Division I volleyball at The Ohio State University, attend law school, become a lawyer, get married by age 25, and have two children before I was 30. Twelve years later, I can tell you that those plans I imagined have panned out much differently. I did go on to graduate high school, and I did indeed play Division I volleyball, but not at Ohio State. I attended the University of Louisville, where I received a degree in sports administration. This path of education led to my current career as a youth volleyball director, not a lawyer. At age 25 I was not married, though I was dating my now-husband. I'm now 28, and there are no kiddos just yet. Why do I tell you all of this? It's simple: Plans change.

Now, I don't want you to take this the wrong way. Plans are good to have. Dreams are important to establish, as they help fuel your soul with inspiration. However, every successful businessperson, professional athlete, artist, and parent knows there is only one guarantee with all plans. Plans change. Period. The person who can accept that is the one who will reach ultimate success and happiness.

As humans, we get so caught up in worrying about things and people out of our control. For example, we spend hours mindlessly scrolling through our social media feeds comparing ourselves to people we honestly don't even like, which leaves us feeling inadequate. Or we allow our minds to be consumed by an ex. We create stories of what they are doing and who they are with that drive us mad. Why? Why let other people's actions and feelings dictate our own happiness? We allow it because we are not at complete peace and happiness within our own selves. When we are not confident in who we are and when we don't have an understanding of what truly makes us happy, we allow things outside our control to control us. Trust me, ladies: a life controlled by others is not the life you want to live. So get in control now.

How do you do that, you ask? Establish your four walls of control. Like a building, you too must have four supportive, strong foundation walls.

163

Four walls of control:

- Your mental state
- Your emotional state
- Your physical state
- Your spiritual state

Your mental state

We've all been there: Your mind is racing in a thousand directions. You can't shut it down. You close your eyes to sleep, yet the thoughts cross through your brain like cars racing through a busy intersection. In order not to let the anxieties of the world, your peers, social media, and so on to consume your brain and fuel you with negative thoughts, you must put your mind in a place where it can't be attacked by negativity. Negativity is all around you, and it will remain all around you if you allow it to. People who do not have a clear head that is at peace are consumed by negativity and concerns about things outside their control.

So how do you keep your mind at peace? It's not easy, especially in a world cluttered with distractions and devices. If it were easy, the majority of the population would already be doing it, and I would not be having this conversation with you right now. So, what is the secret to a calm mind? Discipline. Discipline is something many humans fear and have no respect or appreciation for. In chapter nine, we learned about habits. Discipline is a habit. If you can have the discipline to slow your mind down at an early age, I promise you that you will create a lifetime of overall peace and mental wellness for yourself.

Obviously, this sounds great, and you are thinking, *I'm all in. But how? How do I slow my mind down?* Several steps are necessary in order to fully understand how to bring your mental state to a sense of peace. Writer Robin Sharma puts this process best in his 20–20–20 morning ritual. Sharma explains that in order to bring your mind to complete peace and optimal thinking for the day, you should spend the first hour of your day doing the following:

- 20 minutes of exercise
- 20 minutes of reflection/meditation
- 20 minutes of growth

The 20 minutes of exercise is key; it gets the blood pumping first thing in the morning. This allows blood and oxygen to be driven to the brain, resulting in the firing of neurons that provide alertness, focus, and clear decision-making. Exercise also releases endorphins known as dopamine and serotonin, which are responsible for happiness. The 20 minutes can be as simple as push-ups and sit-ups or a quick run around your neighborhood, any form of activity to get your body physically moving and jump-start your morning.

Next is the reflection/meditation phase of the morning ritual. This is a key part in helping slow your mind down. I personally find it easiest to reflect by writing in a journal. There is an inexplicable sense of calm when you watch words flow freely from your pen as you express your gratitude, desire, even frustration. Seeing these things on paper helps you realize all of your blessings in life and be grateful. It allows you to see your dreams and truly ponder the steps you must take in order to make them reality. Lastly, it helps you to face your frustrations and realize that sometimes they are just simple roadblocks in your life that you hadn't taken the time yet to sit back, analyze, and plan around.

Last is the 20 minutes of growth. Maybe that means reading a book or article on a topic that has had your interest for a while. Maybe it means listening to an inspiring podcast. Whatever you choose, these 20 minutes are designed to help further your brain so that you can become a better woman.

Now, I know what all of you are thinking. *There's no way this BS is going to help slow my brain down! Besides, even if it did, I don't have 60 minutes a day to do all of this stuff. I literally can't even get everything done that's on my plate right now!* I agree with all of you. I thought the same thing when I first learned of the 20-20-20 method. Honestly, I thought I couldn't even go to the restroom without someone calling and needing something from me. However, when I first adopted this method, I was at a point in my career and personal life where I was running on fumes. I was being pulled in so many directions and needed by so many people, and I was completely exhausted. Mentally, physically, emotionally, and spiritually, I had nothing left. I had hit a wall. My mind could not take it anymore. I read about the 20-20-20 method and believed it would be impossible to fit it into my life. Maybe when I was retired.

However, I told myself I would give it a try for 66 days, as Sharma suggests in his book, because I had nothing to lose. After only a week, I was astounded by the results. I never believed a go, go, go type of person like myself, whose mind and body were always on the move, could ever feel a sense of peace and calmness that resulted in happiness. However, I was undeniably wrong. In a week's time, my crowded brain, with racing thoughts crashing into one another, suddenly had a surreal sense of peace and calmness, like a beautiful sunrise over the ocean. The anxieties that had been weighing so heavily on my subconscious had changed into thoughts that I recorded in my journal and action plans I wrote out to address them.

I challenge you to take the same leap of faith that I took when I was at my breaking point. You do not have to wait until you're running on empty. Start now and keep your tank full. Make the commitment to being disciplined enough to eliminate all distractions, including people and devices, for one hour every morning in order to have a healthy and happy mind. Having a mind at peace will allow you to adapt in an ever-evolving world that will throw so many curveballs your way.

Remember, the only guarantee with your "life plans" is that they will change. It takes a woman who is mentally strong, mature, and confident to be flexible and change when plans go awry.

Your emotional state

Gaining control over your mind is the first step to happiness and success. However, a healthy mind is nothing with a broken heart. Devoting time to your emotional strength is important in establishing overall confidence, success, and happiness as a woman.

As females, we are typically more emotional than our male counterparts. There is nothing wrong with that. It's simply how we are wired. The key is knowing how to channel our emotions. As a teenage girl, you are going through so many life changes: puberty, new schools, broken hearts, and back-stabbing friends, just to name a few. Understand that it is okay to have all the crazy emotions that come along with these changes. More importantly, understand that you are not alone. Where you will run into trouble is if you keep these emotions bottled up. Try to find that one person you can express yourself to, whether it is a friend, a coach, a teacher, or a counselor.

Expressing those feelings a little bit at a time, versus keeping them bottled up, will allow you to have a sense of emotional peace. More importantly, it will allow you to have logical control over your emotions. Visualize this comparison for me: Think of a two-liter bottle of Coke. If you shake it up and twist the cap off immediately, Coke explodes and fizzes out everywhere. Now, picture this option: You slowly open the cap little by little over an extended period of time, insuring that the Coke does not fizz out the top. You are just like the two-liter bottle. If you can let your emotions out little by little, over time, to someone you trust, you will never get to the explosive emotional state that's like Coke fizzing out everywhere from a shaken two-liter bottle.

Keeping your overall emotional state at a peaceful level will help you be less reactive in the constantly changing world around you. By opening up about your feelings often, you will be able to think logically when your emotions are running rampant.

Your physical state

The overwhelming statistics of teenage obesity in today's world show a scary reality. Your body is like the dream car you desire. If you don't put the right oil, fuel, and maintenance into it over time, it will break down. Your body is your lifelong means of transportation.

We already discussed the importance of getting your body moving first thing in the morning, but let's take it a step further: Commit to one hour a day, five days a week, of physical fitness. Find something you enjoy and stick with it. Make it a habit. Maybe it is a sport that you enjoy. Perhaps going to yoga with a friend. Joining a gym with your family. The significance is not the activity you choose to do; it's that you choose something you enjoy doing and that the activity is sustainable.

Make exercise who you are, not just something you do. You are not a girl who works out; you are a physically fit girl. When a habit becomes your identity, the chances of you sticking with that positive habit are much greater. As we have discussed, living a life of fitness releases serotonin in our brains to make us feel happy. Physical exercise triggers endorphins in your brain that help with alertness, focus, and clear thinking, all of which will be vital throughout your life when you are dealing with stressors. Exercise will be a key player in helping you reduce anxiety and stress, allowing you to adapt as your plans change.

Your spiritual state

When you lose your mother to cancer and your father is diagnosed with it a year later, when two teammates and their mothers are killed in a fatal car crash, and when a virus takes over the whole world, forcing everyone into quarantine and crashing the economy, what do you do? Where do you turn? *Faith.*

Faith is the only answer. When life keeps punching you in the stomach and beating you into the ground, the only thing you have to hold onto is faith. For many of us, the problem with our spiritual states is that we only focus on them in times of desperation. Our relationships with God are often one-sided. We only go to Him when *we need* Him. We never give anything in return. We never give thanks for our daily blessings. We become so selfish and consumed with our own lives that we forget to show His love and grace to others.

In order for us to experience true happiness and success as women, we must fuel our spiritual states every day. God is our friend. He wants to hear from us every day. Talk to Him. Thank Him. Visit Him. Pray for your loved ones daily. When the world goes dark, hunger fills the streets, and pain crushes our hearts, those who know God will feel His love, grace, mercy, and everlasting peace.

It is my hope that each of you has goals, dreams, and plans that you have set for your lives. I pray that all of you are able to reach these dreams. However, I want you to realize that your plans will continue to change. Life will put up roadblocks in your future, and you will have to find alternate routes to reach your goals. My hope for each of you is that you not only accept that but are able to adapt to it, that you are able to navigate your way in a mindset of peace and positivity. I hope that at an early age you learn the importance of the four walls of control for your life. Only then will you be able to manage your mental, emotional, physical, and spiritual states to create inner peace and happiness for your life.

Summary

- You can create as many plans as you want; however, plans will always change.
- People who can adapt to changes in plans are those who reach ultimate success and happiness.
- Once you stop allowing other people to influence your happiness, you take total control of your own life.

Your four walls of control:
- Your mental state
- Your emotional state
- Your physical state
- Your spiritual state

CHAPTER 18

The Journey

~♡~

"It is good to have an end to journey toward; but it is the journey that matters, in the end."

—Ursula K. Le Guin

Each of us has morals upon which we base our decisions. We also have values, drawn from our families and from the experiences that have helped shape us. In addition to our morals and values, we have personal goals and dreams we wish to achieve. We know who and where we are now, and we have visions of who and where we want to be in one year, five years, ten years, and so on down the road. All of these visions begin with an end in mind, an ultimate destination that we hope to make it to.

There is nothing wrong with having these dreams and visions. However, where many people go wrong is in striving to make it to these destinations without enjoying the beauty of the journey upon which they must embark in order to make it to their fantasy paradise. Throughout your life you will have many different journeys: friendships, relationships, hobbies you put countless hours into as you improve your skills, your high school career, applying to colleges, going to college, obtaining your first adult job, buying your first home, marriage, raising kids, your career, starting your own business. The list is endless.

With every journey can come an overwhelming sense of fear of the unknown and fear of failure. These fears can cause anxiety. Those who choose to approach each new journey with a positive mindset and an appreciation for the process of getting to the final goal are those who, more often than not, reach not only success but true happiness. There is beauty in the daily discipline it takes to finally master that soccer move you have been practicing so diligently. There is joy in the hours upon hours you put in sitting quietly with your own thoughts while painting the beautiful masterpiece you've been envisioning for weeks. There is pure bliss in watching a friend finally walk away from that toxic relationship when you've spent months talking and supporting her through the steps of leaving.

With every final destination, we have preplanned steps we think will take us there. However, as we have discussed before, life throws curveballs at us. Plans change. Obstacles are placed before us. We are faced with challenges. In order to be successful and grow, we must accept and overcome all challenges that are thrown our way, not just the ones we want to. Some challenges will seem more exciting to tackle than others, but we must tackle all of the challenges equally, no matter how big or small, exciting or boring they may seem.

As we face these challenges square-on and overcome them, day by day we grow a little bit stronger. We gain a little more knowledge. We boost our confidence a little bit higher. We become a little bit closer with the people in our lives. We influence someone in a positive way a little bit more. It is through this process of overcoming challenges, growing as a person, and helping others around us that we realize the true beauty of life lies within the journey itself, not at the destination.

As you go through your life, the different journeys you embark on will cause a range of emotions. Some of the experiences will be challenging but the process extremely enjoyable to work through. Others will be filled with grueling pain and heartache, but you will come out on the other side stronger than ever. No matter the nature of the journey, it is important to remember a couple of things.

First, the journey is only a matter of time. It is a route you are on that is based on your own decision-making, and it will lead you to a destination. What that destination will be is all in the hands of the captain of the ship. You are the captain of your ship on this voyage called life. It is imperative that you remember to truly acknowledge the journey you are on with love and appreciation, because it will not last forever. The journey shapes your mindset, builds your character, and molds you into the woman that you are. It is the time spent in the journey that defines who you are, not the destination.

Secondly, there is beauty in every journey; we just have to search for it sometimes. Oftentimes, you will hear people say, "Why do bad things happen to such good people?" People will blame God in times of tragedy or hurt. Many things will happen throughout your life that you will not understand. There will be no words to take away the pain you will feel after a significant loss. There will be times you feel you are in such a deep hole, there is no way you will ever be able to climb out. But it is at the times when we are most broken that we must remind ourselves to see the beauty of the situations we are in. Happiness is a mindset—a mindset that we have 100% control over. When the journey of life gets tough and you feel like throwing in the towel and jumping ship, remember this: No storm lasts forever. The rain will eventually stop. The clouds will disappear. The sun will come out. And you will wake up realizing you have weathered the storm and made it out alive.

You are your own captain. The voyage you are on is your life. You make all the decisions to lead you to the destination. It is my dearest hope that you choose to navigate your ship with a positive mind, a caring heart, and a giving hand. When you learn to approach your life with this attitude, you will see the true beauty of the journey itself, not just the destination.

My Goal-Setting Worksheet

GOALS. There's no telling what you can DO when you get **INSPIRED** by them. There's no telling what you can do when you **BELIEVE** in them. And there's no telling what will happen when you ACT upon them. –JIM ROHN

SHORT-TERM GOALS

ACADEMIC	HOBBY	PERSONAL
1. _____	1. _____	1. _____
2. _____	2. _____	2. _____
3. _____	3. _____	3. _____

LONG-TERM GOALS

ACADEMIC	HOBBY	PERSONAL
1. _____	1. _____	1. _____
2. _____	2. _____	2. _____
3. _____	3. _____	3. _____